LIFE

OF

GEORGE HENRY

LIFE

OF

GEORGE HENRY.

TOGETHER WITH

A BRIEF HISTORY

OF THE

COLORED PEOPLE IN AMERICA.

PUBLISHED BY GEORGE HENRY,

The Black Heritage Library Collection

 BOOKS FOR LIBRARIES PRESS
FREEPORT, NEW YORK
1971

First Published 1894
Reprinted 1971

Reprinted from a copy in the
Fisk University Library Negro Collection

INTERNATIONAL STANDARD BOOK NUMBER:
0-8369-8848-5

LIBRARY OF CONGRESS CATALOG CARD NUMBER:
73-164389

PRINTED IN THE UNITED STATES OF AMERICA

GEORGE HENRY.

A VALUABLE GIFT.

Mr. George Henry, an influential colored citizen of Providence, R. I., has given to Livingstone College, his entire library of choice and rare books. Accompanying this is an oil painting of himself, and portraits of John Brown and Tousiant L'Overture, Charles Sumner and others. Excellent cases with glass doors were also sent and several other articles of value suitable to a nice library. This is among, if not the best gift Livingstone has had from a member of the race. Among these books are several valuable works on the history of the race in the first half of the century. These books are rare and contain much information the present generation knows or seldom hears anything about. Also the entire works of Charles Sumner, twelve volumes, which are very valuable. Mr. Henry deserves the universal commendation of the race for this rich gift to a deserving Negro college.—[THE STAR OF ZION, 1895.]

INTRODUCTION.

I believe in a universal God; for in the heart of man there are universal thoughts between him and his maker. You may lock a man up in his dungeon, and fetter him, yet that freedom will burst forth in a coming day which no day, no tide, can impede, and will roll on and on until the end of time. Therefore I proclaim liberty to all mankind and to the world. Let us rise together and press on together till the great victory which God has given us is won.

Onward the star of civilization makes its way; for I believe that every human being that was born was born free, and there is nothing that ever kept a man in slavery except the army and the navy, for all nations have enslaved their fellow men, even the proud nation America. The Algeries had enslaved the American whites until 1816. They were liberated by the bayonets.

CHAPTER I.

BIRTH OF GEORGE HENRY—ANCESTRY—PARENTS.

George Henry, the author of this work, was born in the state of Virginia, in the year 1819. As my parents died when I was quite young, and there were no records kept in those days, I am compelled to rely upon the testimony of others.

My mother was a mixture of the Anglo-Saxon with Anglo-African, her father being purely African. My father was three-fourths Anglo-Saxon, his father being purely Anglo-Saxon. As I am told. I had not the honor of making any of the bargains, for I am sure I should have made them different.

My mother gave birth to nine children, I being next to the youngest. My father died when I was very young, and his only grief was that he could not educate his sons. He was a strong, robust man, without education, an honest, upright, intelligent man, and a gentleman in every respect. I cannot speak too highly of him, words are inadequate to tell of his philanthrophy and talents. He was an anti-slavery man when anti-slavery was unpopular, and was noted for his physical strength, and also for his untiring energy and ambition in the sphere where God had placed him.

CHAPTER II.

BOYHOOD DAYS.

In my early days there were no schools for those of my class; for it was under penalty of death for any one to be caught teaching the Bible. The poor whites were in as bad condition, as far as education was concerned, excepting the penalty.

I can just remember, one summer, way down in my neighborhood in a meadow, there was an Englishman teaching four boys the alphabet, and the slaveholders came on top of the hill and discovered him, took their guns, crept down upon him and shot him dead. The authorities applauded them for so doing, said they did right.

Now, readers, you must excuse me for not giving day and dates, for you see I had no opportunity of doing so, and can only give you history from memory.

I remember, when a boy, a man by the name of George Thompson, of my own name, provided that at his death mother and her family were to be free, but another man named Camm Griffith, being educated and skilled, still held her in bondage. But I caught the sound of freedom and was determined not to be fettered by any man. He tried his best to make me a dining room servant and wait on table, but having a dislike for that profession he did not succeed. I always had a mind above anything like that. So I studied how to get out of it. When one day he had a table full of company, I blew my nose in an offensive way, and something sticking to the plate that I handed to a guest, he became exasperated, and he highly delighted me by ordering me out ; so he had no further use for me in that dining room.

Numerous little tricks occur to my mind as I write, one of which was, when mother gave birth to an infant, I asked the nurse, where did it come from. She said, out in the "pusley bed." So I set about digging, and uprooted the whole bed without finding one, and when the old lady found me out, she was much enraged at the damage I had done, and drove me away. So I was continually being driven away from all my undertakings.

A man from the Eastern Shore, Capt. Jones, had three daughters, Sally Ann, Rosy Ann, and Julia Ann. They kept store at Norman's Eye Ferry. I had a cousin who came there one day to whip me. Mrs. Jones and the girls took me, hid me behind the counter, and they took sticks and lashed him clear out of the premises, because I was a special pet of the family. So as there was no amusement for me

I erected a swing down under a hill, and it was my delight to swing the girls, especially Sundays, when the old folks would go to church, one or two of the girls would always be sick, and nothing but the swing would cure them. One Sunday the old folks got home rather earlier than we expected and caught us at that, so drove me out of there.

In those days they made the boys, when quite large, wear what they called "Bandauns," a sort of loose frock, and one day the boys all put theirs on and went off, but I determined to wear no such thing as that, so I bundled mine up, carried it down the hill, made a fire and burned it up, but the fire got away and they found me out, and had to go down and put it out, threatened to whip me but they did not. So they drove me away from there.

They tried to get me to nurse the children while the women were out to work, another occupation I always hated. So I studied how I should get out of that. I got a pin and tormented the child so bad they drove me out of that, and declared I should never mind any more children of theirs. I was determined to do none of their mean, low, occupations around houses. I aspired to something higher.

CHAPTER III.

White-Bread, Travel, Horses, Etc.

In entering upon the third chapter, when about fourteen years of age, old people used to tell me when I would be kicking up my heels and playing: "Ah boy, you are eating your white bread now." I then did not understand what they meant. Full of enthusiasm, I longed to visit other cities, to see the great men, hear them talk, and inform myself thoroughly of the peculiar features of civilization. But so many years ago travel was only the lot of a "favored few." My body was fettered but my mind was always free and aspiring.

My next occupation was that of a hostler, caring for and driving horses, an occupation that seemed a little above the others, but that did not satisfy me.

I was placed under a man named James Wood, a great hostler and driver. I served at that about two years. During that period I had a great many falls, from being thrown by horses, but I got so at last that no horse could throw me. One horse in particular we had, he did'nt want anybody to ride him. He would stand right up and throw them off. One day he was so determined to throw me off, he stood upon his hind feet as streight as a man and fell over backwards. I sprung from him, and before he could recover his feet I was on his back again, and he never tried that trick with me again.

I would never ride any but the best horses. I went to the camp ground once, and there were a lot of horses, the people wanted us boys to drive to water. I picked out the largest, best black horse, he stood about six feet high. The watering place was a mile off, and there was a crook in the road. Before he got there he commenced to run away with me, and instead of turning the crook he ran streight into the woods. I hauled his head clear around to my left leg, which was the means of saving my life. The first tree we came to I dodged it, and the second tree, his head took the blow first, and we both fell. they all thought us both dead, and it was so reported at the Camp Meeting. I was carried back insensible, and knew nothing of the circumstances till late in the afternoon. The doctor bled me, and every drop of blood was black as a man's hat, and clotted. I was removed from the Camp Ground home, and never came out of the house again for three weeks. I was just as anxious to ride a horse as ever after that, and continued so for awhile. At last I got tired of horses and began to grow restless for something higher. The "boss" found that out and was determined to satisfy me if possible. So he gave me the keys of the meat houses, dairy and all the out houses, and made me overseer of everything on the place, supposing that would satisfy me, a duty which I performed faithfully to a letter, and whatever plan I laid out, he never was the man to oppose or find fault with, I laid them so deep and skilfully. I worked when I pleased and let it alone when I pleased, but I hardly ever knew what sleep was, and those who were under me had to be on time night or day. There was no idle bread eaten where l was. I had from twenty-five to thirty hands under me, and could have kept two hundred employed as well as them, when comparatively but a youth. No one could have supposed one so young could have managed business so well.

I continued this command between two and three years. I was always ahead of time. One morning I called up all hands about two o'clock, supposing it was day, and put on a ring of wheat and eight horses, and took off the first coat of straw about sunrise, a thing I never shall forget

CHAPTER IV.

EFFORTS TOWARDS FAME AND GLORY.

Seeing vessels often coming into the harbor, and talking with the sailors, brightened my hopes of a better future than the dark and benighted ages in which I then lived, and in the words of Hon. Charles Sumner: "No honest, earnest effort in a good cause can fail." So I determined to make that effort, and thought best to go by water and widen my ideas of civilization. So the "boss" under whom I was working built a vessel on purpose to satisfy me, knowing that he would never be able to subdue me to the occupation I was then working at. This vessel was built on Strother's Point and was called Llewyllen. The builder was named Goggins, from the Eastern Shore. She was caulked by Mr. Abrams, of Baltimore, the best caulker I ever saw in my life, and when launched they sent to Baltimore to get her spars and second-hand rigging for to take her to that city to get her new outfit. I enlisted as cook, under Henry Weaver, her commander, the first captain I ever sailed with, also a crew of four others. I was just getting in my glory. I could see something of the outside world, without being shut up in one place altogether. Loading we started on our journey to Baltimore. So we came out of the creek, down to Potomac, round King Copsica Point, all the way down to Point Lookout, into the broad Chesapeake Bay. Everything went on smooth and nice and to me everything was lovely. We sailed on that day till we got up near Hill's Point, and went under there for harbor. There came on a gale. We expected every moment to be lost, and would have been, but providentally, we had on board a new caboose, which we rigged with a new hawser, and threw overboard. It dragged until it buried itself entirely in the mud, and every sea washed over the deck. There could'nt a man stay on deck. The Captain at one time said he did'nt see any hope for the vessel or our lives. I began to think my days were numbered, and that I had just got in the wrong place.

After the gale was over, and we easily regained the anchor, but the caboose was hard to get, and we thought at one time, we should have to leave it, but that was the article that saved our lives and the vessel. Two days we could cook nothing, and we subsisted only upon "hard-tack." At last we succeeded in getting the caboose, and the cooking process went on, to sustain the cravings of nature. We made sail and wafted our way on toward Baltimore.

Before reaching that port we got up to Poplar Island, we met another adversity, of head winds, but not so severe as the first. I began to think we were having a hard time. When near Annapolis Light we were near running into a vessel. However we escaped that, and still "onward" we made the Bodkin Light about 2 o'clock P. M. There Capt. Weaver showed us the Point where Ross, the English officer, landed to take Baltimore. And he told us that Ross said he would eat his dinner in Baltimore that day, or eat it in torment. He did not succeed, and was killed. So we must think he ate his dinner in the latter place. I shall always remember that circumstance. Our tedious journey ended about five or six o'clock that day ; we reached Baltimore. Pardon me, for I have no means of giving dates, but our first voyage was between five and six days.

We landed our cargo, which consisted of wood in the hold and timber on deck. The Captain then commenced unstripping the old rigging and sails, to have her rigged to his own liking, from top to bottom. While this was being done I took the opportunity to go all through Baltimore, making observations of what was going on. There I saw an accident such as I never saw before nor since. A new steamer was just about to start on her trial trip down the Bay. Just as all hands got on board ready to start, her boiler burst, and from twenty to thirty persons were mangled and killed, in the most shocking manner, bodies flying about in every direction, and the steamer was blown to pieces.

After being fully rigged in the best manner, we started on our return voyage, arriving home safely, a wiser man, with knowledge to impart to friends, and with double zeal to increase my knowledge of the world.

CHAPTER V.

CONTINUATION OF SEAFARING—SECOND VOYAGE, ETC.

We loaded with wood and timber for Philadelphia and sailed on till we came to Bodkin Light, and N. N. E. till we got to the head of the Cheseapeake, thence through the locks of the Canal to the Deleware River. Being a novelty, when I first got into the locks, when they raised me up and down, I did not know whether I should ever get out of the locks again or not. I found the Deleware River a new atmosphere, and when we got in Philadelphia I found there was something in the outside world I had'nt seen. I took a tramp in this strange city and saw many new things I had never seen before. Among those which attracted my attention much was the statue of William Penn, who I was told was the founder of that great city, and was the Indian's friend. On my return home I had a new panorama to unfold to my friends of this great city, the land of the free and the home of the brave. Then I began to consider seriously the declaration of the rights of man, believing that God made these hands and these feet for George Henry. Upon this declaration

my mind was made up. I intimated to my friends
that I would make Philadelphia my adopted home.

My next voyage was to the Navy Yard at Washington, with timber and wood. Upon arriving there
more strange scenes presented themselves, and I
began to find out more and more of the world.
After being unloaded, the tide made against us, and
being in a strange place, the Captain told us boys
that we might go up to see the Capitol, the centre
of this so called free country. I had heard of it
before, and my eyes longed to see it. On our journey, under the hill of the building, we heard such
screaming and crying, we could'nt tell what it meant,
so we kept on till we met about two hundred men
and women chained together, two and two, and there
was some as pretty women and as fair as the sun
ever shone upon, also the men. I, being a green-
horn, asked what does that mean? They told me
they were being taken down to Alexandria to one of
Armfield's vessels, (he had a regular line and slave
pen), for New Orleans, to be sold into slavery, and
sir, the scene was enough to bring tears into any
man's eyes if he had a heart. When I saw that virtue was to be sacrificed to the highest bidder I said
then "Away with your pretended free America, it is
all a sham in my eye." It was then and there I took
an oath against slavery, and that I would never go
to Washington, unless I went with an army to take
her or burn her down. Just as we left the Navy

Yard there was a large ship blown up by a torpedo, placed under the water, the first I ever saw. Four men steered the ship until she got nearly over it, then took boats and left, and when the ship got directly over the torpedo, they sprung a mine and blew her clear up out of the water. This was done merely for experiment. On arriving home, I still had more fresh news to tell, and so ended my trip.

CHAPTER VI.

The Black Jaws of Death.

My next voyage, we loaded again with grain and started down Chesepeake Bay, encountering a terrible gale in passing the Horse-Shoe, being blown off our course clear down to Cape Henry, but we got through safe and entered the river, a very crooked river. We sailed right by the place where Gen. Butler cut through, now called the Dutch Gap, and the river was so crooked I thought we never would get up to Richmond, and when we did arrive I saw a great many colored people, but they all seemed afraid to speak to me. So I walked about town that day as big as any other man. I did'nt care whether "school kept or not." I observed they all kept an eye very strictly upon me, but not one said a word to me during the day.

When night came the Captain sent me up town after some things, and I always thought he laid that plot in order that some one might tackle on to me, because he knew if they did there would be "death in the pot." On my return down street a watchman hailed me. I sang out with a double oath, "What business is it of yours?" He said it was his orders to take anybody up that was out after dark. So I swore an oath that if he did take me he would have to take me dead. So when the watchman found he had to eat blood pudding before he did take me, he calmed down and talked as pleasant as a man courting a woman. We talked awhile as friendly as could be. He told me about the town, the usages of the town, and what was the law there, and told me not to get angry at what he said to me, he was only doing what he was ordered to do; that the captain of the watch was a nice man, and was always friendly to sailors. So we walked along down the street till we came to the watch house. Now, said he, "just step in and speak to him and that is all that is required." Soon as I got in the key was turned upon me and there I had to stay all night. I swore enough to sink the city, if that would have done it. That was the first and last time a man ever fooled me, for I cut my eye-teeth fully.

Next morning I went down aboard the vessel, and the Captain asked me where I had been. I ripped out an oath and said, I suppose you know where I've been. I was a pretty ugly fellow all that day, just hoping the Captain would say a wry word to me, and the feelings I had toward him. I never got over it.

We got our stores aboard and made sail for home. We made one or two more trips to Alexandria after that, and I told the owners I was dissatisfied with that Captain and would'nt sail under him any longer. My reason was that I thought he did that on purpose, and I never would be satisfied with him again. When they found there was no such thing as retaining my services they turned out Henry Weaver and gave me command of the vessel myself. I had sailed under him three years. He had no learning more than myself, and none of the skippers had any learning. It did not require it to run up Chesepeake Bay and Potomac River.

As I left Richmond for the last time, 1 pronounced its doom as follows: "Let darkness and judgment cover the place. I'll never return again 'till I come with fire and sword to burn it to a dross." And that prophecy has been fulfilled.

CHAPTER VII.

ENTERING ON A NEW CAREER.

Here I first entered on my career, with all the persecution that could be heaped upon me, no one to give me words of cheer. Had I been weak and timid I should have sank under the persecution, but with courage bold I marched on in my own way towards liberty and civilization; for I felt that no power could stay my progress, and this is the true course of all true-hearted men. Let the watchword be ever "onward."

After arriving home I took charge of the schooner Llywellen. I have no opportunity of giving you dates. William Weaver and John Palmer sailing out of the same river at the same time, they being noted skippers, the latter one of the finest captains out of that creek. They were all down on me, and said the vessel was lost; I would never be able to run her in the world.

My first voyage was to Baltimore, loaded with timber. Arrived safe and delivered. Second and third voyages the same. Making shorter and quicker voyages than any other skipper that ever went out of that river. They began to think their prophecy would'nt come true, but for all that they would talk against me. The more they talked the harder I drove them. Finally I made two trips to John Palmer's one. He was sailing the schooner Independence, belonging to John Rice.

I did'nt know what sleep was day or night, for after I had charge of the vessel, I was determined to let them see that though black I was a man in every sense of the word. My fourth trip was to Alexandria, with wood, and the first cargo I sold to Stephen Shinn, and the next to William Ramsey, two of the most noted wood and grain merchants in Alexandria at that time.

As I would sail down the Potomac, past Fort Washington on the left, and Mt. Vernon on the right, where lies the remains of the immortal George Washington, where my grandfathers fought side by side in the Revolutionary War, with the soldiers of the country, under the pretended flag of freedom, for no other purpose than for the declaration of rights and liberty. I could not look on that spot with reverence, as I should look, because he did not announce freedom to every man, when the bloody struggle should be over, but slavery continued worse and worse under the reign of Washington than it did under the reign of Great Britian. The chains grew tighter and tighter, until at last the General Assemblies began to pass statute after statute in nearly all the Southern States, to drive out the free colored people. Owners of property amounting to from twenty-five to thirty thousand dollars, compelled to sell it for five or six hundred dollars, and were robbed out of all their property, amounting to millions, besides being obliged to leave the State in so many days or be made slaves. All this was done to please the slaveholders. Now I ask the reader at large, is it any wonder that we should be poor men? Virginia announced in her constitution that "All men having sufficient evidence of permanent common interest with and attachment to the community, have the right of suffrage, without distinction of color, and that they cannot be taxed or deprived of their property for public uses, without their own consent." This was entirely worthy of the citizens who adorned that State. In the early history of Virginia, 1723, on the enactment of a statute, she undertook to disfranchise people of color, but was rebuked by legal authority in England, in admirable words as follows : "I cannot see why one freeman should be used worse than another, merely on account of his complexion.

I want my readers to distinctly understand that there were as many white slaves as there were blacks, and rather more. King James emptied his prison houses and they were transported to Portsmouth, Virginia, and sold as slaves, to work out their sentence. This was carried on until December, 1620, when the Pilgrims landed upon Plymouth Rock, a period of sixteen years, and the following April one-half of that number were dead, and only seven able to work. Just at that critical moment, when everything was about to fail, there were forty-five Africans landed upon the shores of Virginia, and from that time to the present you have heard no more of starvation, and the country has been on its solid march, through and by the labors of the Africans. Now, I wish it distinctly understood by my readers, that the record of the landing of the Africans upon these shores is as clean as a hound's tooth. Every man had the right of suffrage, until after the declaration of Independence, and the Americans had the reins of government in their own hands. So we were not only robbed of our property, but of our franchise, under this system of slavery, which no government ever upheld or sustained, by a positive law, but the Americans.

Georgia, in 1777, formed a constitution confined to male white citizens, and in 1798 adopted another without the word "white." It only remains to speak of South Carolina. It was the only state which after uniting in a National Declaration that all men are "created equal," openly commenced the example of a white man's government.

I now refer my readers to the arts and sciences of the ancient colored people who were the leaders of civilization of the world, at the time of Hamilear 250 years B. C., who carried on the war with the Romans, till his son Hannibal, who at the age of nine years, swore on the altar of his country, eternal hatred to to the Romans, an oath which he kept till the day of his death. His perilous ascent of the Alps, 200 years B. C., up to that time the Carthagenians, who were the leaders of the world, but have lost their power since the death of that great hero, whose daring feat never has been equalled by man, or never will be again, according to the historian. And all the great achievements in the United States have been carried on by colored people, for which they get no credit.

CHAPTER VIII.

OTHER VOYAGES AND OTHER STRANGE INCIDENTS.

My next voyage was to Annapolis with a load of bark, sold to a man named Hayden. Arrived there on Saturday, not time enough to unload. So on Sunday his body-servant invited me to attend church. I saw a great many different things I never saw before. While in church I saw a young lady named Kitty Dean, with whom I fell deeply in love, and asked the young man her name, and if there was any chance of getting an introduction to her before I left the City. He being well acquainted with the minister, he planned to have the minister's wife invite her the next evening, also the young man was to carry me up unexpectedly, not to let any one know. Our plans being deeply laid, Monday night, the eventful night, there came up a terrific thunder storm, with rain in the streets nearly half a leg deep. It broke up all our plans, and Tuesday I had to sail for home. But I always believed if I had got acquainted with her, I should never have gone home again. I had many strange tales to tell, because I had been in another strange place.

By this time the owners had made a large contract to ship timber to Baltimore. My attention was called to that city for some time carrying timber. This contract made me quite an expert in getting out ship timber. After the first contract was filled, the following winter I had a gang of hands and went into the woods to pick out ship timber. If I put my eye on a piece of timber that was suitable for breast hooks, beams, keel, keelsing knees or beams, it had to come down. On the second contract, one dark night during one of my voyages down Chesepeake Bay, wind blowing very hard from the eastward, so that vessels could just lay their course up and down, sails all set. I had been at the helm all night. About three o'clock in the morning I let go the helm and went forward to see what was going on. The first thing I saw was a large powerful ship bearing down upon us. I sung out to my man "up helm," and the ship put "down helm," and we just grazed one another. If I had not gone forward, which I think was the providence of God, she would have run over us, and we should never have been heard from in the world. My watchman was asleep, and I gave him one of the greatest duckings any fellow ever had. He never went to sleep on watch again. When I related my hair-breadth adventure, the people at home rejoiced with me that we so narrowly escaped a watery grave.

For a period of a year and a half I did'nt run any

more timber to Baltimore. Just at the finishing up of the second contract, the "boss" engaged another contract to run all the piles to build an aqueduct across the river at Georgetown, which could never be built without those piles being run first. The piles were to measure from forty-five to fifty feet in length, very straight oak trees. Soon as the vessel laid up that winter, my business was with a gang of hands, picking them out and cutting them down, and another gang hauling them to the water, ready for shipping in the spring. That was my business every winter till the contract was filled. In the spring every one was landed at Georgetown under my command.

The engineer of the aqueduct, named Major Turnbull, was the prettiest and the smartest engineer of his time. So if my readers will visit Georgetown you will find that what I tell you of his history will be facts.

It will surpass the ideas of any man, unless he could be on the spot, to see how it was done—to know how men could go down to the bottom of that river and work, the same as on the highway. Now sir, I could take a gang of hands, if I could be supplied with all the material, and build just such piers as those, across Narragansett Bay, because I know just how that was done, and no power of ice or wind would ever carry away one of the pieces, or ever want repairing again.

About this time the schooner Llewylen had carried

so much heavy timber, night and day, that she was nearly used up. I then said boldly to the owners, that I would'nt go any longer without I had a new vessel. So he told me if I would finish out that season I might go in the woods the following winter, take a gang of hands, and get out all the timber I wanted, to build a vessel the next spring. I took him at his word and made the next trip to Baltimore, landed my cargo, and on my return home, just below Poplar Island, wind blowing very heavy, carrying full sail, I sprung my foremast, and had to take in foresail, got a deck-stay on my foremast to keep her from going overboard, put my foresail down two reefs, and the bonnet out of my jib, and took a reef in my mainsail. The sea was setting on so heavy that I was afraid she would go overboard. I had to carry that sail, for it was life or death. If it had been otherwise we would have gone on lee shore, and the vessel and all hands would have been lost. We turned Point Lookout between three and four o'clock in the morning, and had fair wind right up Potomac River. If there were ever glad hearts they were to be seen that morning, when we turned Point Lookout, for the wind was increasing to a gale. Next morning we made King Copsica Point, and arrived home about mid-day, after a night of severe trial.

CHAPTER IX.

NEW VESSEL—OTHER VOYAGES AND ADVENTURES, WITH HAIR-BREADTH ESCAPES.

I was compelled to make my next trip to Alexandria, because my foremast being partly sprung would not permit my going into Chesepeake Bay. The owners had a mast made against my return from Alexandria, so I rigged my shares in the morning, took out my foremast, unstripped it, put the rigging on the new mast, set it in, and had everything completed by next morning ready for loading.

It was considered by all the skippers out of Norman Eye Creek that I completed that job quicker than any other skipper that ever sailed out of there, for when there was a foremast or mainmast to be taken out or put in other vessels, it always took other skippers two days to complete the job.

I loaded up for Baltimore with timber as usual. After delivering my cargo, returning home, wind blowing heavy to the eastward, entering Norman Eye Creek about daylight, having been at the helm all night, the channel being crooked and difficult coming in, I let go the helm to go forward to look out for a small buoy, and the fellow "up helm" rather too soon and the foresail jibed, the wind blowing heavy, I standing in front of the foremast just as it jibed, and the jaw rope of the foreboon broke, and the end of the boom shot by the mast and struck me just on the cheek bone, I fell as a dead man, and all thought I was dead, and I did'nt know anything till we got up to Norman Eye Ferry, where I was taken ashore and placed in care of a doctor, and with good care soon recovered, having lost only one trip. Had to get Henry Weaver to take a load of wood to Alexandria. On his return I went aboard and took charge again, fresh as ever.

I then went on to fulfill the contract to Baltimore, with the balance of the timber. Autumn was now drawing very near, and we would'nt venture to Baltimore any more that season.

One more trip was made to Alexandria, and on our return home, we laid up a little earlier that season because we wanted to go in the woods and get timber for the new vessel. I had fifteen hands cutting down, hewing out timber, and digging up roots for clamps. Two setts of whip-saws (for sawing out plank and timber), going all winter. Two setts of teams hauling down to the shore all winter, and we got out timber enough that winter to build the vessel and complete the contract to Baltimore.

About the first of February we commenced building the vessel. She was built right at Norman Eye

Ferry, by a man named Gaggins, from the Eastern Shore. She was not built as vessels usually are, in a "cradle," but on "skids," as the water was very deep, and she was launched sideways. The vessel was completed that summer, and her name Susan Ellen. You will find them both recorded in the Custom House at Alexandria. I brought rigging, anchors, and a rigger, from Baltimore, also brought second-hand sett of sail to rig her temporarily to take her on to Baltimore, to fit her out in her new suit. We arrived in Baltimore about the middle of September of the same year, and rigged her out as fine as a schooner could be rigged. I took a delight in having everything put in firstrate order. I had main sail, foresail, square-sail, jib, flying-jib and main topsail. I was determined to have her fitted out in flying colors, because I began to make up my mind not to wear her out as I did the Lewellyn.

Just before I quit the Lewellyn, I came home from Alexandria one afternoon late, and I went to Dr. Murphy's where I supposed I had married a woman who would have been some use to me, named Annie Gordon, daughter of Betsey Parker. I did'nt eat any dinner aboard, and it was so late when we got in I would'nt commence loading that afternoon. I supposed I had a wife and a home. I sent for her to get me some supper. It was getting late and I was quite hungry. Just as she got my supper pretty well under way, her mistress sent for her, and said she must wait upon her first. I had to do the best I could, but it was the first time I found out I had neither wife nor home. I made up my mind then and there. I had two children by her, a girl and a boy. I said to myself, madam you may have your woman and her children. I will never work myself to death to raise children for your use. I never revealed the secret to any living being on earth, what I intended doing. I made out that I was delighted with my new schooner and new situation. The owners thought I was perfectly contented and there would be no more talk about quitting. I kept on making regular trips as usual, trip after trip.

The winter following, the owner got another large contract for timber, as I bore the name of an expert in getting timber. My usual manner was to lay off timber enough to employ the hands three or four days at a time. I was also considered a great gunner, and after laying off this work, I would go a gunning three or four days. The owner found the acquipments and was to have half the game. In those days it was against the law for a colored man to carry a gun, but I carried one regularly every winter, and sometimes killed so much game that I could'nt bring it home, had to leave it on the shore. The biggest shot I ever made was eighteen ducks at one fire. I used to go off, two miles from home, and stay a night and a day gunning. I gave out my proclamation, that if any man love that gun better than his life, he could take it away from me. I would have shot him quicker than I would a duck. And there never was a man that attempted to molest me with a gun. But any other colored man in that neighborhood, caught with a gun, would have had the life chased out of him.

During this period I was a very profane man, uttering oaths at every word, and was called the king of Devils, also a great dancer, and continued dancing one night until Sunday morning dawned. Once having to pass through a skirt of woods about a mile wide, at three o'clock in the morning, the girls all remonstrated against my starting for home till daylight. But I being very venturesome would'nt hear to them and started off. It was the first time in my life I ever got scared. When arriving about midway in the woods I saw something look white, like a sheet, so I had my dirk open in my hand and started boldly towards it. It wavered and wavered, as though it was most up to me, and I got so scared that my hands fell paralized and powerless. I was too "spunky" to run and kept my eyes right on it, and walked right up to it, made up my mind better die than run. But when I got up to it I found it to be a large whiteoak tree that had been cut down and stripped off for tan bark, and become dry, and it being damp that night everything else looked dark around, except that which had a white look, so I got up on it, sat up on it, and rolled on it, for a quarter of an hour. After that nothing could scare me. I was "boss" after that.

Another time I came home from Alexandria, no one knew I was in the river. I heard of the girls being at a dance and I went there, stationed myself outside till the dance broke up, so as to have some fun with the girls, as they were going home. As soon as the girls came out, I ran ahead of them and got to a place said to be haunted. I got one side of the road, pulled my coat up over my head, and stretched myself on my hands and feet, and made two groans as the girls passed by. They started and outran a horse. When they got home, they burst in the door and fell in top of one another speechless, and when they came to, they told the folks they had seen a ghost with no head on, and heard him groan. One was bedridden for two weeks and the others liked never to have got over it. I went aboard again and staied all night. Did'nt dare to let it be known that I was ashore, or they would have declared I was the ghost, as I was up to all such tricks. The next day when the news got out that the girls were scared to death with a ghost, I was the sorriest man around there, and abused the young men for letting the girls go home alone. If I had been there I should have seen them home. They never found out but what it was a ghost. I made up my mind I never would do such a thing again, though it was "all in fun."

CHAPTER X.

SKETCH OF MY HISTORY WITH SALLY GRIFFIN.

I will here give you a sketch of my history with Sally Griffin, to let you know that I was a man. She lived in Alexandria, on King street. She and her nephew owned the schooner Lewellyn, that I was master of for ten years. She was built on Strother's Point. After I wore her out, had another one built, the Susan Ellen, and I was making money for her, just the same as if you were shaking it off a tree. I went up one day in a hurry to pay her the money and she knocked my hat off, and I declared by all the Gods in creation that she should never take another cent out of my hands. I knew that I was going to Baltimore the next trip, with a load of grain, and I was determined she should never take another cent out of my hands. When we carried a load of grain it was always consigned to commission merchants, because they could get more for it than anyone else. When sold they take out their commission, and the balance was handed over to me with the papers, and they did not dare to hand it to anyone else except me or the owner of the vessel.

I knew that the vessel and cargo was entrusted into my hands. I could wait till the cargo was sold and come away with $1800, as well as to come away without anything, but I was too much of a man. I secured every cent of their property and they got it all, I felt that I was a man. Never wronged anyone of a cent that I knew of. So I took George Henry's property, which was one suit of clothes and fifty cents in his pocket, and came on to Philadelphia, where I shipped with Capt. Bayman, for nine dollars a month. I went with him about three years. The next captain I went with was Capt. Hawkins of Long Island, next was Capt. McKenny of Providence, the next was Capt. Fowler, and the last I went with was Capt. Nickson of Cape Cod.

I want to tell you one of the prettiest sights I ever saw, when I sailed out of Philadelphia, the wind stayed east for over a week. The vessel would come up to Deleware and load and then come down to Marsh River and anchor there, and wait for the wind to change to westward, so we could come on to New York. When the wind was to the eastward there were over one hundred sails in sight. I was then with Capt. Baymore in the schooner Ninneeta. The morning we started we got down as far as Barnett, half way to New York, and the wind changed and blew a living gale, and scattered the fleet in every direction. We were driven to sea, and I thought my time had come. I had given up all hopes of seeing home or land again. When we got down in the brough of the sea it would seem as if it was impossible for the vessel ever to come up again. We did not get into New York for nearly a week, We should have got in the same day, had we not been driven out to sea. Some of the vessels were lost, and some got to New York through a great deal of difficulty. I have often compared that voyage to the christian pilgrimage. They are scattered all over the world, and if they are born of the spirit of God they have got to come from the east, north, south and west, and enter in at the one gate, whose maker and builder is the living God, where God and Christ has aloted for all His childred, just the same as those vessels were driven whither and thither. They were bound for New York with their cargo, they must land there and no where else. This is a great lesson for christians to study.

Now I want to ask this enlightened world if they will state the exact color of Adam, as he was the only man that God created, as he and Eve were the only two that God ever did create. So we have the color from the lightest to the darkest shade. Who is it that has changed this color? I hold it was God himself. I will tell you of a case that I know that happened in Alexandria, the upper end of King street. Armfield was a regular inland slave trader, run slaves from Alexandria to New Orleans, he had two vessels in that employment, when one would leave Alexandria with a load of slaves the other would leave New Orleans to get a load of slaves. This I know. I have passed them more times than I have got fingers and toes. I have been unloading wood on one side of the wharf when his vessel has been loading slaves on the other side of the wharf. He and his wife lived at the upper end of King street, and his wife had twins, a girl and a boy, and they were as black as lamp-black. They were chained together with a fine link chain, but yet it was flesh. In those days they called the mid-wife. The case was such that she could not manage it, and they had to call in the doctor. He had to cut the chain, and the children died. The circumstance was shut out from the public, so that it did not get into the papers. This was a judgement sent upon him from the Almighty. So be careful how you tamper with the Almighty's works. It is Him alone that changes those colors, so be careful.

CHAPTER XI.

CONVERSION, BAPTISM AND CHRISTIAN CREED.

I run the new schooner only about two years, and during that period nothing particular occurred about the voyages to cause them to differ from others.

I always used to like to attend meetings, but principally for the purpose of plagueing the girls. One man named Edmund Tate, one of the greatest preachers I ever heard. He was a perfect gentleman and a christian—lived it every day. Through his preaching I was convicted, and the doctors could'nt tell what was the matter with me. I expected every moment that I should die—continued that way some length of time—and the moment that I expected I was going to die I gave up everything in this world, then I became truly and soundly converted, then everything was new, even my flesh on my bones was new. "My glad soul mounted higher, in a chariot of fire, and the moon it was under my feet." The very man I had sworn before to kill was the first man I tried to persuade to join with me. Most of my comrades turned in and were truly converted, and like Paul, when he was going to Damascus to bind all that called upon the name of the Lord, and bring them to Jerusalem for punishment, and afterwards became most zealous in preaching Christ and Him crucified.

My eldest brother, one of the most pious men that ever lived, without being a christian, when he used to hear me swear so hard, tried to persuade me to better things. So when he stood outside and heard me talk, he just found out that he was a sinner.

I was baptized at Norman Eye Ferry, together with about fifty others, most of my comrades, in the month of December, when the water was very cold.

I, as an individual, make no difference whether a man is immersed, sprinkled or dipped. I believe true baptism is of the Holy Ghost. It is argued that John baptized Christ in the river Jordan. I am told by historians that river is only about two and a half feet deep. Now I should like for any man to answer this question: Is it true that Christ went down into this water and came up out of it? Did John immerse, sprinkle or pour water on Him? Please answer that question. That will settle all difficulties. Now I say "ye must be born of the Spirit and of the Holy Ghost," before you can enter into the kingdom of Heaven. What is the meaning of John's baptizing in the wilderness? for we must acknowledge there was no river nor ponds there. We think he must have either sprinkled or poured. So, in the case of the eunuch, there is no positive statement given, whether she was sprinkled, dipped or poured upon. In my judgment it is useless to argue these points, as there is no positive proof.

I take up the Saviour's argument, "ye must be born again," and if a man never saw water, his way is clear. For there is only one church, namely, the Church of Jesus Christ. Those taking the opposite view please answer these questions.

Now I come to reflection. I am about to fulfill the promise I made a year or two ago. When I knew I was to make a trip to Baltimore, with a load of grain, my mind was made up. I went around and paid up all my debts. I never let any mortal know what I intended doing. When we loaded with the grain, I said "good bye" to the land of bondage, I am now about to sail for the "land of the free and the home of the brave." Our little vessel wafted over the deep blue waves, until she reached the shores of Maryland, where I had landed many a cargo before, both of grain and timber. But I said in a still small voice, this is the last cargo I shall ever land from the schooner Susan Ellen. No one knew the secret save Him, who said, "let there be light, and there was light." Freedom's land I was bound to see. We arrived in Baltimore safe with the vessel and cargo. I had a new hawser on board, and I tied her up with three strands double. She never would have got from the wharf till the hawser rotted.

Always when I carried grain either there or to Alexandria, it was consighed to a commission merchant. Because they could get the highest market prices. Always first carrying a sample to the commissioner. The vessel was subject to his removal, and when the grain was sold, his fees taken out, the balance of the money was handed over to me. I always paid my bills, got my stores, paid the hands, and paid the balance of the money to the owners on my return home. If I had been mean enough I would have waited till after the cargo was sold, taken upwards of eighteen hundred dollars, and went away as easy as I did. Gone into Canada and set up business "on my own hook." But there was too much manly principle within me to consent to do such a thing.

But I had considered and knew that these hands and these feet belonged to George Henry and nobody else. I told my mate that I was going up town a while, and if the commissioner came down and wanted the vessel moved, "You move her, wherever he tells you." I knew he was responsible for vessel and cargo, and that the owner would get every cent of the money and the cargo too. The only trouble would be to have the owner send on a captain to take the vessel home. So the owner nor anyone else could never say I wronged them out of the sixteenth part of a cent. I was determined that his property should be safe and sure. With that assur-

ance I stepped ashore, determined never to put my
foot on her decks again.   I traveled on till I got to
Havre de Grace, arriving there about night.   Paid a
boy fifty cents to run me across to the Pennsylvania
side and took the cars for Philadelphia.   No man
ever said a word to me during the whole period, until about leaving the cars to take the boat for Philadelphia, one man said to me "where are you going?"
I answered him sharp enough to cut his head off.
Said I, "What business is it of yours where I am
going? That is not a question for you to ask a
gentleman." Finding I was in a passion he immediately asked my pardon, saying he meant no harm.
He was going to Philadelphia himself, and as he
apologized we became very great friends. We arrived in Philadelphia about eight o'clock next morning, and this man gave me considerable information
about the city, for which I was very thankful.

I was now alone on Free soil, with the wide world
before me, to look out for myself as any other freeman.   I at once went from vessel to vessel look out
for a berth. Found none that day, and as night
drew on, I made inquiry for a colored Baptist Church,
as I was a member of that denomination I supposed
I would be perfectly at home, if I found the deacon
of said church.   I was shown where such a church
was, and my next enquiry was for a deacon belonging to said church.   I was directed to one that resided close by the church.   I supposed after dis-

closing my condition to such a one, I should be in the arms of a christian brother. But alas, I was deceived. Most bitterly deceived. On arriving at his house I found only his wife at home. I told her my situation, and that I did'nt want to put up at a boarding house, and only wished to stay with a friend all night. She thought if I waited till her husband came, I could be accommodated. The deacon arrived about half-past seven o'clock. I made known my desire, and stated that I was a member of the Baptist Church, and did not want to go among strangers. He gave me to understand there was no room there for me that night. He dragged me off to a boarding house that was full, and they could'nt take me. He then dragged me across town to another boarding house that was full. We returned to his house, and he was discussing the question with his wife, where he should carry me that night, and she rose up in the power of her christian might and said, "Brother, you shant go out of this house this night. I will make a pallet right here on this sofa, if you can lie on it." I told her I was perfectly willing to lie on the floor. So the old iron-heated deacon's guns were silent, and the angel of the covenant had spoken her voice. She made me a pallet on the sofa, and I never slept better in my life. Early in the morning I rose and asked her what she charged for my lodging, and she said : "Not a cent, my brother. I am glad I could accommodate you."

I thanked her kindly and shook the dust off my heels, against all Baptist deacons after that. I thought he had neither heart nor principle, let alone being a christian. But 1 want her name to be coupled with Mary the Virgin. I don't know her name, but I want that act to be handed down as long as time shall last. It is also my wish that all the female sex of the world may be kindly treated. I think they deserve it.

CHAPTER XII.

Onward Freedom! to freedom's land,
Onward Freedom! forever stand,
Onward Freedom! let man stand and die,
Freedom! forevermore.

After leaving the good woman I went down upon the wharf, seeking for the first time my own living. Onward, onward, my mind flowed heavy to commence my career for freedom. Freedom! that word was locked up in the heart of man, guided by the Redeemer, who "ruleth all things well." I succeeded in securing a situation with Capt. James Raymore, who kept a store corner of Front and Christian streets, Philadelphia. He also kept a large wood yard adjoining the United States Navy Yard. Coming down from my lofty position as captain, I was obliged to ship as cook. For as I came North I found prejudice here greater than in the Southern States. I had to content myself with nine dollars a month as steward. But with all this I felt the proud dignity of manhood about me, and was determined to take up with anything that had money in it. The stewards around there begged me not to go with

him, for they said he was the severest captain about
there, that there never was a steward sailed with him
but he whipped him before he got back.   But I had
engaged to go with him, and "my word was my
bond."   I said if he whipped me, they never would
see him or me in that port again in this world.   I
got all my stores on board, ready for sea, the next
day.   About two o'clock we made sail down the
Deleware River, for Fall River, Mass.   There came
up a heavy squall in the afternoon.   The captain
cursed his "hands," sung out, "take in that fore-top-
sail, brace up main-topsail, take in your flying-jib,
and take down a close reef."   So I began to think
what the boys told me was true.   I braced up and
said to myself, if you declare war, I am ready for the
conflict.   But he never gave me a wry word.

The next day about eleven o'clock we made Cape
May, and put to sea at once.   We had a terrible
rough time.   We were three days and nights before
we arrived in port.   I kept good courage, and we
arrived in Fall River, delivered our cargo, got stores
aboard, and returned safe to Philadelphia.

I should have mentioned that we called at New
York City and took on board a load of merchandise
for Philadelphia.   We unloaded and cleared up
everything, and thus ended my first voyage in
freedom.

I told the captain, as I had only shipped for one
trip, we would settlé up and I would look for another

berth. He asked me why I wanted to quit him. I told him I thought I could do better, and I did'nt think he wanted my services any longer. But he prevailed on me so hard that I consented to make another trip with him, this time to Newport, R. I. It was now late in autumn. I have not opportunity of giving dates. Arrived in Newport late at night. When I came on deck to get breakfast in the morning, I thought I never saw so deserted a place. I could see nothing but rocks and leafless trees. For curiosity I went to the captain, and said "what place is this?" He said Rogue's Island. I said "this is the last place God made, and He made it out of the scraps." It amused him mightily, and he told his wife when he got home, and she came near cracking her sides with laughter. After that they gave Rhode Island the name of "Scraps."

I reshipped from Philadelphia for Providence. On our voyage we met a desperate time. We started to come in Sandy Hook about three o'clock in the morning, in a very heavy rolling sea, and the captain sung out "all hands on deck!" It was my watch, and two hands below at that time. We sprang upon deck. Everything was washing overboard. I being very venturesome, sprang forward to help shorten sail, and she shipped a sea just at that time, and washed me clear overboard, and she having a high waist, I caught my left hand under the gunwale and as the sea lifted her and she rolled, I sprang on

board to the windward and got in the rigging.
There we hung, not daring to move. It was im-
possible to do so. Eevrything washed clean off the
decks. The captain found no chance of getting in
Sandy hook, for she would have foundered at sea.
So he squared off for Fire Island. We made the
"Light" just about daylight. So we put off, gave
her good sea room, run down on the back of Long
Island till we came to Montauk Light, and we got in
the river time enough to make harbor that night.
Next morning we weighed anchor and got up to the
City. But we were pretty well racked, and the captain did'nt know of my getting washed overboard
till I told him of it next day. We unloaded and
made for Philadelphia again. Another time we were
coming into Sandy Hook and a vessel ran into us
and came very near sinking us. Our trip then was
for New York. Returned to Philadelphia, loaded up
and started from there of Friday. On the following
Sunday the great riot broke out between the Catho-
lics and the Protestants, on account of the priests
wanting to take the bible out of the schools. The
Captain's wife came on with us that voyage. The
vessel "Ninetta" was named after her. We arrived
in Providence on Monday, and when the Captain's
wife took up the paper, and saw where the riot was,
she was like a crazy woman. Because it was a terrible riot. There were no quarters shown on either
side. She was much afraid some of her children

would get killed. But it so happened that they were conveyed off to a place of safety. About half a block from her house, a man went to poke his head out the window to see what was going on, a ball struck and killed him instantly, and in the store corner of Front and Christian streets, where the Captain kept his meats, there was a ball found in one of the hams, from that riot.

I continued to sail with Capt. Baymore between three and four years, and I never sailed with a better captain in my life. He never gave me a wry word in the whole of that time. Every winter he used to trade South, and wanted me to go with him, but I refused him, because they would always take the stewards out and lock them up, till they got ready to sail. I told him if I went and they ever attempted to do that way with me, they should never bring me away alive. When I made that final declaration he never again asked me to go South with him.

I was compelled to board during the winter in Philadelphia, and it took all my summer earnings to keep me through the winter. The first winter that I stopped in the city I went frequently to Bethel Church, of which Rev. William Moore was pastor, and I found out he was a gentleman and a christian. After relating my circumstances to him, I made application to join his church, and was admitted a full member. Rev. David Ware was my class-leader, and continued so during my sojourn in Philadelphia.

When I found out by trading East, that there was a line running from Providence to New York, winter and summer, I made up my mind to leave Philadelphia, and establish my headquarters in Providence, because I could save expense. So when Capt. Baymore laid up that winter, there was a four top-sail schooner, named John Jay, running a regular line from Providence to Philadelphia, and I found out by waiting her arrival, I could get free passage back to Providence. I waited two or three days, something she had never done before, to be so long over her time. Something impressed me not to wait for her, but to go on to Providence by rail. I said I would wait one day longer, and if she did not arrive I would take rail, and I did so. It seemed as if something was driving me out of the city. So I took the cars next morning at seven o'clock, arriving in Providence about night. Took boarding-house in Chickenfoot Alley, with a man by the name of Lang Weeden, and I was so fortunate as to get a berth next day in the sloop Juno, Capt. John G. Allen. We loaded up and went on to New York. We lay in Quince's Slip. There came on one of the severest snow storms I ever knew, much as we could do to lie in the slip. The John Jay arrived in Philadelphia the day after I left, and loaded up for Providence. She came down the river out of Cape May, and in the same gale I speak of. She has never been heard of from that day to this, not a piece of her. It shows you that God did not intend I should be drowned in that vessel.

I took my letter from Rev. William Moore, Philadelphia, and joined Bethel Church, Providence. Francis Jackson being my class-leader, and should have always been there if it had not been for S. S. Lewis, a man that was unworthy of a name, let alone being a minister. And as I wanted to live in peace, as a christian should live, I left peaceably and joined St. Stephen's Church.

I sailed in the Juno, between Providence and New York, about one year. In that time I learned the Sound pretty well, so I quit him, not for any reason whatever, he was a very fine captain, but I thought I could do better.

CHAPTER XIII.

"Come forth, historian of our race,
    And with the pen of truth,
Bring to our claim, to manhood's rights,
    The strength of written proof.
Draw back the curtain of the past,
    And lift the ages' pall,
That we may view the portraits grand,
    That hang on history's wall!"

Onward I went to Mr. Whipple, in Providence, to
ask him for a schooner, which he had laid up at the
wharf at that time, to run coal on shares, from
Roundout to any port wherever I could get the best
sale. But alas, 1 was refused, and upon no other
ground than on account of his not knowing me. I
wondered then if this was a free North. I was then
compelled to go back to my old stand of being steward. I shipped aboard the sloop Radiant, Captain
Hawkins of Long Island, and still run between Providence and New York. During this time I made a
trip to Albany, and I drew a map from Albany to
Providence, with all the lights, cities, towns and
harbors, and when I showed it to the Captain, he

did'nt believe I could have drawn it. Somehow or other I got it misplaced, but I would'nt have taken a great deal for it.

I remained a little over a year with Capt. Hawkins, and quit him because I did'nt like him. Then I shipped in a schooner with Capt. Isaac Johnson, that sailed out of East Greenwich. He was in company with a man named Pierce. I made several trips with him, to different ports, for about a year. I had no fault to find with him, he was a very nice man, but I prefered to sail out of Providence. Then I shipped in the schooner Darius, with Capt. Nicholson, from Cape Cod, a line direct from Providence to Boston. We used to lay at India Wharf. One time while we lay there, they brought in a large ship, which lay close side of us. I think her name was Panther. She had a large black Panther as her figure-head. She was caught in the slave trade.

The third voyage with Capt. Nicholson, I married a widow, of Providence, named Mrs. Hester Jones, living on Williams street, between Brook and Hope streets, on the spot where a new double house now stands. The original having been torn down to give it room. She was the mother of two children, one named Eliza Jones, and the other a boy, named Ellsworth Jones, aged respectively six and eight years. It being the last trip to Boston that winter, I married her like tonight and left about three in the morning, and did not see her again for a month.

She was a member of Bethel Church, and as fine a woman as ever stood in shoe leather. She was gentle and kind, and desired to make everything and everybody happy around her. She did all in her power during the time she was with me to make me happy and comfortable. She was like the woman spoken of in the Proverbs. She would "rise early, and her candle goeth not out by night. Her children rise up and call her blessed. Her husband also and he praiseth her. Many daughters have done virtuously, but thou excellest them all." After our marriage, in due time, she gave birth to two children, named George Edward Henry and Frederick Henry, both of which died in infancy. One lived one year and one month, the other only one month.

I remained in Providence during that winter, and did'nt get a day's work to do. I contented myself, and made myself quite happy with my new wife, and when spring opened I shipped again with Captain Nicholson. We loaded up and started for Boston. Went over the Sholes about night, but before we got around Cape Cod we encountered a terrible gale. No more idea of seeing land again than I had of flying. About three o'clock that morning the captain about gave up all hope of surviving. But by the providence of the Almighty we weathered the storm, and got in a harbor about four o'clock in the morning. A place I never was in before. I did'nt know where I was, but the captain understood the harbor well, as he was an old coaster, and knew exactly where he was. We furled our sails, and all hands went below to take a nap, as we had been up all night. We rejoiced that we had escaped a watery grave. We slept rather later than usual next morning. When I got up to get breakfast, there was not a drop of water around the vessel within four hundred feet of us. I thought we had escaped one danger and got into another one, and we never would get out of there again. When the captain came on deck, I said to him : Captain what does this mean ? He laughed and said we'll get away from here bye and bye. But I thought differently. So we got off deck and went digging clams. We brought the clams on board and had a grand time eating them, and throwing the shells overboard. After a while the tide began to come in, and soon we saw the flat fish coming round eating those clam-shells. In three hours from the time that the tide began to rise, the vessel was afloat. I never saw so many flat-fish in my life, some of the largest kind, and the bottom of the sea was literally covered. So we got a gig and went to work on them, and caught from two to three hundred before we weighed anchor. We made for Boston, and had fish enough to last us nearly a week. Arrived safe in Boston, after a dangerous and perilous voyage.

We loaded up and put back again for Providence, arriving safe, loading the second time for same destination, sailed down Narragansett Bay, stopped in Newport all night. Next morning put for Gay-Head, came near running on "Sow and Pigs." If we had we should have gone to pieces sure. I began to think that an unlucky route—accident both ways. We went on however and anchored in Hyannis that night. The captain went ashore to see his family, as they resided there. He always made it his business to stop at Hyannis coming or going, to see his family. I always made it my business to loosen the sails, "heave short," and get ready for a start. It pleased the old man well. I never liked to lay at anchor long myself. Got under way next morning, went round the Sholes, and put out for Boston. Arrived, delivered our cargo, returned to Providence. After sailing with him the remainder of that year, about December first we laid up and I quit him.

Then I returned to my old route, namely, New York, in the sloop Oregon, with Capt. Kit Fowler, who belonged in Wickford, R. I. I used to go in harbor at that place often with him. Sailed with him during that spring and summer. The winter following we were caught in a very severe snow-storm and gale, in Stonington, all hands on deck, expecting to go ashore on the rocks. She was dragging both anchors, going as hard as she could, a heavy sea setting on, and Capt. Fowler gave her up. Says he, "Boys, we are all lost tonight. There is no possible chance for us to be saved." I said to him: "Sir, you are captain, but if you will give me my way I will save the vessel tonight." I remembered the circumstance that happened to me when I made my first voyage. So I got the caboose and hawser, made fast to her and threw her overboard. Doing same as I did with Capt. Weaver, in my first voyage, and saved the vessel. We paid out the full length of hawser, and when the caboose got hung in the mud, it brought her head to the wind, and she never dragged again till she rode out the gale. Captain Fowler was frank to acknowledge that if it had'nt been for me they would all have been lost that night. After the gale was over and we went to get our anchors, we had the same trouble to get our caboose as at Hill's Point. We weighed anchors, went on to New York, unloaded and loaded up for Providence.

I continued a year or two with Capt. Fowler, and found him a very fine man during my voyages with him.

CHAPTER XIV.

ANOTHER VOYAGE AND OTHER OCCUPATIONS.

But yet onward, onward I still wandered over the dark blue sea, seeking for treasures, as all men do. Press forward! whispered the sweet voice. Such is the road to honor, virtue, righteousness and wealth.

I remember one of our voyages. We started from Providence at three o'clock in the morning, arriving in New York at eight p. m., a distance of nearly two hundred miles, which was considered one of the quickest voyages ever made by a sloop. The wind was blowing heavy to the eastward, and we carried a whole mainsail, squaresail and topsail. I must say with all my voyages, I never had a prettier run in all my life. Capt. McKinney was the most careful and safest man I ever sailed with, excepting Capt. Beymore. I should have staid with him longer, but I quit him upon principle. He took a stray boy on board from New York, and wanted me to wait for my meals till he got through, and I would'nt do it. So I quit him for good after that.

These voyages with this captain was about the winding up of my continued seafaring life. Although after settling down to shore life I made several voyages, at intervals, during the winter, and in summer took charge of St. Stephen's (Episcopal) Church, of which Rev. Henry Waterman was rector, corner of Benefit and Transit streets, in this city, where I remained upwards of twenty-five years. During this period the Society built a new and substantial edifice on George street, modeled after Dr. Waterman's own taste. He, together with his father, spent a fortune to carry out his designs. He continued their rector until a very short time previous to his decease. He was a man of ability and great power. He not only preached his religion, but lived it daily. I also worked for his father, and found him also a christian and a gentleman. I want his name to be honored and cherished, as a memorial, henceforth and forever, to all generations that shall come hereafter.

I found prejudice so great in the North that I was forced to come down from my high position as captain, and take my whitewash brush and wheelbarrow and get my living in that way. My first work on shore was at Mrs. Patrick Brown's, 45 Williams street, that of digging a well. When I got through with that she employed me to do all her work, until her death, twenty years afterwards. During that time I also worked for a colored man living on Benevelent street, named John Johnson, whose business was watering streets. He employed me at a dollar per day, to pump water to water the streets, which I pumped from daylight till dark, a very laborious work. That was considered great wages in those times. But I was determined to work, knowing it was my living, and I had to support a wife and two children out of that.

I worked thus one summer, and my attention was next called to the cheapness of land hereabouts, and I tried my best to get up a combination of colored men to buy up the land on east side of the bridge, which if they had listened to me then, they could have monopolized all the east side just as well as not. My attention was next called to a co-operative grocery store, which we did establish. Some five or six persons raised one hundred dollars, and with as fine a prospect before us (as we thought) as any set of men ever had, and was doing a flourishing business. We selected two as honest men to carry on the business, as we thought were in the city. That one hundred dollars turned over, according to the books, eleven hundred dollars. But I lost every cent of my enterprise, as did the others, excepting the two that we placed so much confidence in. Now I say if we had had honest men, as we supposed, we would have been as rich a firm as any in the city. So you see where confidence first began to weaken. So I say to all persons, when confidence is once betrayed, never trust them again under any circumstances.

My next enterprise was: I came in contact with a

man who had nine lots, and houses on all except one. He was an aged man, having no family, and was anxious that the colored people should have the property. He would let me have the whole of the property for ten thousand dollars, part payment at first, and turn the rents all over into my hands. Not being able to take it myself at that time, which I knew was one of the best bargains that any man could offer to another. So I appealed to the colored men of this city, and more especially to the Society to which I belonged. I could'nt get a man to help to secure that property, but rather to the contrary. They did'nt want it, had no use for it. In twelve years time from that date the same property could'nt be bought for forty thousand dollars. Now I ask, in the name of Heaven, is it any wonder that we are such poor and degraded people as we are?

So I struggled on and never got discouraged, knowing what was in the grasp of man. After a lapse of time, through my ardent persuasion, I got six men besides myself, to put in eighty-four dollars apiece, to start another firm in the grocery line. We planked five hundred and eighty dollars cash, and selected two more men, whom we thought were as honest as the sun, to carry on our business, and it was carried on flourishingly for a year, and then that busted up, and I never got the sixteenth part of a cent, nor did either of the five who constituted the firm. Only the two that we placed there, who ran away with every cent, and every particle of the goods. Now where can confidence be established? I don't think with me it can ever be established again. Now I say sir, until confidence can be established amongst us, we must make up our minds to be hewers of wood and drawers of water for all generations to come.

My attention was next called to the caterer. I saw at a glance that the colored people could monopolize the whole city in the catering business. I never was nor ever wanted to be a caterer. But we had one here named Burrill, one of the finest in the world, and I saw it was necessary to sustain him and hold up his hands. So through my strong efforts I called a meeting in the lobby of the Old Baptist Meeting House, "on the hill," for the purpose of permanently establishing him in that position. My proposal was for him to select a half dozen of the best colored waiters in the city, and they should bind themselves to be ready at his call, to wait upon any party or gathering. And my idea was for each of those men to pick out four or five honest and upright men, and make them pledge themselves to be at their call, to wait at any gathering. I thought by doing this the catering machinery would be in perfect order. I still believe if that idea had been carried out, that the colored caterers would have been in the place of Humphrey and Ardoene today. So they may blame themselves for being in their present sad condition.

CHAPTER XV.

Watering and Cleaning Streets.

My attention was next called very forcibly to the cleaning and watering of the streets, which at that day was a very profitable business. There were six or seven watering carts, all owned by cololed people. We had one man here, very smart and energetic, named Joseph Gardner, who got up a small engine to pump water to save labor, and none of the other watering carts would patronize him, simply because there was no union. And here at this stage I interfered myself, and used all the influence I could bring to bear to unite those men in a body, so as to be able to build themselves up in the future, and they would have been able to monopolize that business forever. But I could'nt possibly get them to see the point, and so it failed, and threw all the business in their hands, and Mr. Gardner not being able to carry on the machinery it went down. Here was one of our great downfalls, through our own neglect. So they worked on in this hard way until water was introduced into the city. So I say now boldly that we have had the best chance of being the richest colored people in the New England States. But the great prejudice to one another has caused us to be as we are, and if it cannot be broken in any other way, let us pray God to send an angel from Heaven, that he may reveal unto every man's heart, to do away with this prejudice from amongst us. Then, and not till then, will we become a united and a thrifty people. confidence must be established.

In the year of our Lord 1855, I turn my attention to the subject of public school rights. I find myself paying a heavy tax, and my children debarred from attending the schools, for which I was taxed. So a few of us got together and resolved to defend ourselves against such an outrage. Mr. George T. Downing was the leading man in the first part of the campaign.

The first petition was to break up the colored schools, and let the children go into the different ward schools. Upon that I bolted, and declared I would never sign my name to any such petition, because I did not believe we had any right to break up that school—told him so—and that upon that plank they would whip us, and they did. We were left with not a single plank to stand upon, and all said they would never agree to break up a school that their forefathers worked so hard to establish. So the next year my proposal was to petition the General Assembly that my child should go to school in my own ward, where I pay taxes and vote. So when that petition went in, our opponents had not a plank to stand upon, we swept every plank from under them, and I signed every petition after that until we gained the equal school rights eleven years afterwards. I made converts wherever I went by putting themselves in my place.

We had a very severe contest, but we were determined never to give the struggle over till victory was gained. When we started the battle, nine-tenths of the population was against us, ministers and deacons of churches, and what was more grinding to us, two-thirds of the colored population was against us. About the seventh year of the contest, Geo. Head opened his rum shop on South Main street, and invited all colored people who would remonstrate against the bill to come into his place and drink free rum. And the day the bill was to come up in the House he brought up over one hundred remonstrants against us. That day I lost my balance. I followed him and Davis out of the Court House, down the hill, and if he had opened his head I would have killed him dead on the spot. We were defeated, but we continued on year after year. John H. Clark, of Williams street, who went two or three times to Congress, was bitterly opposed to us. I pitched into him, handling him with "red-hot tongs," So we were at swords points two or three years. But when he saw the injustice he was doing us, he turned and was one of the warmest friends we had. Gen. Greene

was also against me. Every place where I worked
they were against me, and begged me to leave the
field, and I could have everything I wanted. One
said, "Henry, you had better leave the field or you
will loose your bread and butter, and the d—d niggers 'wont thank you for it afterwards." I told him
I was'nt fighting for the niggers, only fighting for
principle, and when he heard I was dead, he might
know I had quit the field. Every one that I worked
for threw me out of employment except Mrs. Judge
Ames, but that did'nt stop me. During this time
John Waugh accidently got his son Frederick into
the district school, and there was such a time made
about it that he was turned out in a little while.
Then we were determined to try the law. So we
begged Mr. Waugh to let us try his case. In laying
the case before lawyer Blake, who said he would try
the case for two hundred dollars, one hundred down,
and if he lost the case he would'nt demand any more.
We raised one hundred dollars and placed it in his
hands for trial. When he came in court Judge Shaw
non-suited us, upon some petty technical point,
without giving us a hearing. That blow discouraged
a great many of our men, but the women came up
with fresh courage, namely Mrs. Mary Ames, wife of
Judge Samuel Ames, Mrs. John E. Church and Mrs.
Mary A. Waugh. The battle waxed hotter and
hotter, till we finally won the day. So let the women
have a name in history's fame. We finally triumphed

on that glorious day of liberty, eleven years petition for Equal School Rights, April first.

In 1870 we petitioned the Honorable General Assembly to repeal that section relating to "Equal School Rights," and it was referred to the Judiciary Committee. They failed to report on it. In 1872 I published a pamphlet, which cost me forty dollars out of my own pocket, entitled the "Final Appeal," requesting the committee to report, favorable or not, a copy of which I laid before every member and clerk of the General Assembly. After that they reported every year promptly until the final triumph. This is one of the questions in my pamphlet which I asked Bishop Clark, of Rhode Island, and he has'nt answered it yet, viz.: "Which seems the most like christianity and humanity, running the ignorant and down-trodden into heathenism, or gathering up the lost sheep of Israel and educating them, and adding them to the flock of Chrict? and as you stand at the head of the Church of Christ please answer that question." The Roman Catholic priests in the South gathered up the poor, weak, down-trodden slaves and educated them, to make useful citizens of them, and the Protestants, with Bishop Clark at the head, run them off to Africa and made slaves of them. This was the cause of my asking the question.

CHAPTER XVI.

SERVING ON THE JURY.

The colored American has ever been loyal and ready to die if need be at Freedom's shrine. The love of country has always burned vividly on the altar of his heart. He loves his "native land, its hills and mountains green."

In A. D. 1872, I was elected jurior in the Supreme Court, in Providence, R. I., and served thirty-three days, from April 22d to June 7th. When I was first called to act as a jurior, Mr. Burgess was my foreman. He rose and shook me by the hand and welcomed me to a seat by his side, and throughout the time I was with him treated me as a christian and a gentleman. During that time there were three sets of juriors discharged, and I alone was retained.

One of the most important cases that came up for trial, which I will mention here, was the noted case of Mr. Casey, a wealthy but elderly gentleman, and a blooming young lady as ever man laid eyes on— held the Court three days. During the time I watched the young lady closely to see if I could detect anything that I thought was unladylike and unworthy of due respect, and I saw nothing but the manners of a perfect lady. She sued in the lower court for $8000 damage, and it was decided in her favor, and he appealed to the Supreme Court. She then sued for $30,000. At this time I happened to be elected on the Grand Jury. When the court ended, and the Judge gave the case to the jury, the sheriff locked us up in a room, for every man to decide for himself how much she should or should not have. And there did'nt a man speak a word to each other but wrote the amount on a paper what they thought she should have, and ten out of twelve said she should have the whole amount of $30,000, and I feel proud that I was one of the ten, for it was the clearest and most just case that ever jury sat upon. So we bothered the second time, and there were ten out of twelve in her favor, the evidence being conclusive that she had been wrongfully treated, by having been to great expense in making preparations for the wedding. After a great controversy between us, we balloted the third time with the same result. Then we demanded to know of the two opposing ones, what was their reason, and neither could give any reason. We then agreed to compromise, and every man put down on a piece of paper what he thought she ought to have, and the two would'nt agree to that. Then we dropped down to $16,000, and one hung out to the bitter end. His only reason was, that he thought it too much money for a poor girl to have at one time. So we ten bore right square down on him, and he had to give in. We thought better do that than to break the jury up, have another trial, and run the risk. We then brought in a verdict for $16,000 for the deserving lady, and I as one felt it to be one of the proudest acts of my life.

During the balance of my stay there we had some criticle cases to decide, but in all cases I always cast my ballot with the affirmative, except in one instance, the jury stood seven to five, and I was with the seven. My last foreman was Mr. Stokes, of the firm of Stokes & Leonard, meat and produce dealers, and I served my time fully and got my honorable discharge, and Mr. Stokes shook my hand and told the Clerk of the Court, that I made one of the best juriors he ever knew.

The promises and obligations of marriage at the present day differ from those of the past, because even in my day the slaves stood more upon the principles and virtues of marriage, than the people of the latter days. The marriage vow was held very sacred. Where there are now one hundred divorce cases, there was not one among the people of those days. Why is this? Moses said it was on account of ignorance that he gave them a writing of divorcment then. Now we have the light of the gospel, which should guide us in the path of righteousness. Let what may occur, a man should love and respect his wife and family, and seek not for a separation except for the crime mentioned in the Scriptures.

The first miracle performed by our Saviour was at Cana, in Galillee, at a marriage. St. Paul then picks up the subject and says, "marriage is honorable among all men." Therefore about the year 1870, we struck that sacred key-note, and commenced agitating the "intermarriage law," in the State of Rhode Island, which we thought was unjust, and an outrage upon humanity. When we looked over history, and found that law was placed on the Statute Book in 1784, by such men as Capts. Gibbs, Scott, Townsend and others, slaveholders of Rhode Island, we had a bitter contest against it, year after year, for Rhode Island had at that time sixty-five slavers, running out of Bristol, Newport and Providence, doing nothing but running slaves, on her import and her exports, and thousands of our colored women's virtue was sacrificed, and fell victims under that law. So we were determined to fight it out till it was repealed. Year after year we were defeated, but kept on. Every year when we came up with the petition, the question would arise on every hand, Do you want your daughters to marry a negro? So in 1879 the Journal came out in bitter tones against us. There was'nt a day but she had the marriage law or the color line in her papers. The colored people were roused to the utmost. I published a card in the paper, that it was'nt the color line or marriage question that had aroused the people, but it was the abuse in the House, that we had received from some of our Republicans. I made a little mistake in my card and the Journal refused to publish anything by way of rectifying my mistake, and I was forced to apply to the editor of the "Evening Telegram," and he was kind enough to open his column for a fair fight with the "Journal," and it was admitted by all that I whipped them fairly on race and color. I published a pamphlet entitled "An Address to the Hon. General Assembly and to the Editor of the 'Providence Journal,'" which cost forty dollars. I did'nt care if it cost one hundred, so as a black man could silence the editor of the "Journal." The marriage law was repealed March 17, 1881, by the following vote in the affirmative: Messrs. C. Anthony, J. Anthony, Bates, Bowen, Brownell, Burdick, Burrington, Carpenter, O. Chace, B. S. Chace, Chester, Chickering, Clark, Crandall, Davis, Eames, Freeman, Giles, Gregory, Jenckes, Lapham, Lee, Mason, Pendleton, Pendergast, Sanborn, Sheffield, Shove, Spooner, Stearns, Stone, Taft, Tallman, Thomas, Tounsend, Vincent, Stilman White, Daniel Wilkinson, Winsor—forty.

The following in the Senate: Ayes—Lieut. Gov. Fay, Senators Babcock, Bourn, Chase, Crandall, De Blois, Greene, Handy, Lyman, Maglone, Moies, E. C. Mowry, J. W. Mowry, Razee, Seabury, Smith, Tillinghast, Watson, B. F. Wilbur, G. A. Wilbur—twenty.

CHAPTER XVII.

PAPERS AND SOCIETIES.

Now let us talk about papers and societies. I have not the dates before me, but there was a paper started called "North Star," the editor was Frederick Douglass, and one started by William Lloyd Garrison, called "The Liberator." They were the only two papers that were able to fight the slaveholder. When Fred Douglass' paper was in its height, fighting for the liberty of the black man, the slaveholders offered $7,000 for his head. I took his paper until the great battle of slavery was over. This country will never produce but one Fred Douglass. They did not get his head. They had to lock Garrison up to keep them from getting his head. But Summers head they did get, from a blow from Bully Brook of South Carolina, which carried him to his grave. He suffered all this for the black man's liberty. Should we not feel proud of such defenders of liberty.

I joined the Young Men's Friendly Assistant Society in 1840. It was one of the most flourishing societies of the day, and I paid into that institution $84.00. The money was for sickness and burial.

I never drew but one week's pay for sickness, and the officers raised a conspiracy and robbed the society out of every dollar. I belonged to the Franklin Lyceum twelve years. I paid three dollars a year membership, and that went down and I lost all that. I belonged to the Rising Daughters of Zion quite a long time. I was one of the committee to draw up the constitution, and was a full member till we dissolved. I joined the Union League right after the war, for the express purpose of discussion how the Southern States should be constructed. No one could come to those meetings unless they gave the right signal. We wanted none but true republicans to decide that question. There were several propositions put forward, some of them were separate government until they could behave themselves and be taken back into the Union peacefully. My proposition was to disfranchise every man forever that took up arms to break up this government, and every man that was forced into the rebel army and proved, he should have right of franchise forever, and hang all the brigade. I still believe that would have been the best policy.

Here comes up another policy, that the loyal black could be trusted with the safety of the country, more so than the rebel. This policy was debated for some time, and I for one heartily endorsed it. So the League adopted that policy, and it was a grand policy. If we could only have had true and honest leaders, of the republican principle, but we failed in this respect, with both black and white, so the government failed in this respect.

I am a member of the Park Association, paying a dollar a year, getting nothing to help secure all the park for the benefit of the public.

Leu Fenix and myself started Burnside National Guards. We waited upon Captain Doyle, who then had a restaurant at the foot of College street, and we told him we were meeting up on High street, at a hall just above the Hoyle Tavern, and we told him what evening we would meet, and that we would have all the boys there so we could organize. In three weeks he had three companies over run, and I was appointed committee to get the army on Meeting street, and when the three companies marched down Broad street, it astonished ererybody, and we had a picked staff, under the command of Captain Doyle, one of the finest commanders that Rhode Island ever produced, but when we came under State laws the officers had to make the measure and through trechery of the officers they made Brown measure instead of Capt. Doyle, and it was so disgusting, they have never had as fine a staff since. The staff immediately disbanded. I was one of the members of the staff.

There were two inferior schools, one established on Meeting street, on the east side, one on Pond street, the west side, and the children were never known to get any higher than spelling. Miss Sarah Brown and myself came together and talked considerable about the condition of the children's education, and we thought it a great pity that they should grow up in such gross ignorance. So we made a firm resolution to try and better their condition. So we resolved to form a society called the Henry and Brown Society. Our idea was that all who joined the society and had children, whether girl or boy, and they got through spelling, this society was to send them abroad and give them as good an education as could be gotten, and then they were to come back and take the other children out of the schools and give them as good an education as he or she had, so they could start fair in the world. After the schools were opened to all we turned the society into a beneficial society. It was formed in 1859 and it is in existence up to date, 1893. Capital of $400 or $500 at this date. It was chartered by the General Assembly on the eighth day of March A. D. 1871.

CHAPTER XVIII.

Our Country and Homes.

It is the bounden duty of all teachers, preachers, and of all fathers and mothers, to teach the rising generation to respect their country and their homes, and to teach them to become good citizens.

In order to be good citizens the mothers and fathers should keep their children in from night scenes, for this is the first step to virtue.

There is a social equality among the colored people which they must observe. Those who wish to have respectable and happy homes, must not admit bad men and bad women—they must make a distinction between good and bad people. If you want to lift up your homes intellectually and morally you must make your homes pure. In order to do this mothers must teach their children, in the nursery, to fear the Lord, because she is the moulding of the nation. The eyes of the Lord are in every place beholding the evil and the good.

The home is the nursery of the colored race, and just as your home is, so will the race be. This is not only true of the colored race, but of every other race. It is in the home that the destiny of a race is fixed. If fathers and mothers wish to know when they are dead and gone, that their children will grow up to be good men and women, let them make their homes pure. Two great factors in the development and growth of the children, are the school-house and the church—the teacher and the preacher. They can be very helpful to the parents. There are men in the pulpit who ought never to have gone there. As long as bad men preach to you, you cannot make the distinction which has already been pointed out to you—you cannot make your homes pure. Blessed is the man who hath a virtuous wife, for the number of his days shall be double. A virtuous woman rejoiceth her husband, and he shall fulfill the years of his life in peace.

The colored people ought not to sit down in church and listen to a man preach who does not live right himself, and whose life is impure. Neither should they let their children go to school to a teacher whose life is not what it ought to be, and no man should be allowed to teach in the public schools who has not a good character for God always blesses truth and virtue.

Education does not mean exemption from work. It should fit you to go out into the world and discharge your duties better as citizens. Let fathers and mothers, and teachers and preachers, put into the minds of the colored children, that it is work from the cradle to the grave—that work is honorable. Any sort of honorable work is honorable in all men. Hear ye children the instruction of a father, and attend to know understanding. For I give you good doctrine, forsake ye not my law, and God will bless you. This is the doctrine that should be preached from every pulpit, and from the fathers and mothers from around the fireside. These ideas can be carried out by saving your money and buying land to build these little comfortable homes. This can be done by learning all kinds of mechanical trades, the same as the whites. You must learn to be doctors, lawyers, farmers, house-carpenters, brick masons, and all branches of machinery, civil engineering, and educate some for the ministry, on the highest culture. If a young man wants to aspire to be useful to his country, let him aspire to civil engineering. That is one of the highest branches, and the most useful to a young man. Then study wisdom which comes from the Lord, with him forever, who can number the sands of the sea, and the drops of the rain, and the days of eternity. This is what young men should study, and God will give them wisdom to carry out all their plans. Now it has been said in former days, never mind the girls, but give the boys education. This is a mistaken idea. The girls should have the best education and culture in the world. The words of the king : "thus his mother taught him, for she opens her mouth with judgment, she is like the

merchant ship, she rises, also she plants the vine-
yard, she girdles her loins with strength, she lends
her hands to the spindle, she opens her mouth with
wisdom in her tongue is the law of kindness, she
lays hold of wisdom." So mother teach your childred
from the cradle up to manhood and womanhood to
be kind and pleasant to everybody.

Behavior is pleasant in all daily walks, in lying
down and rising up, thus you gain the respect of
everybody. Now let the girls be taught that they
are part and parcel of this government, and mothes
should teach the girls all household cares, and when
children come from school always find something for
them to do beside run the streets. Find out what
occupation the girls like. Let them study all branches
that any other lady has ever studied, and when employed, take as much interest in your employer's
property as you would in your own. Let truth and
principle be your motto, and lay hold of wisdom for
your guide, thus you will gain the favor of your
neighbors and your country. Save your money and
respect your country and you will be able to build
these comfortable homes.

HISTORY.

AN ADDRESS

To the Hon. General Assembly of the State of Rhode Island, of 1880, and to the editor of the Providence Journal, on the repeal of the law prohibiting the intermarriage of whites and blacks, by George Henry, Providence.

PREFACE.

This law was repealed March 17th, 1881, by the united efforts of our colored clergymen, in behalf of the people.

The strong arguement of Walter B. Vincent, representative of Rhode Island. So long therefore as slavery existed unrestricted there seemed to be no occasion for the prohibition of marriage between blacks and whites, but the passage of an act in 1784, providing that all children of African descent, born thereafter should be free gave rise to, and was soon followed by the passage of an act which has remained upon our statute books to the present day, and was both in spirit and language the same as the section now under consideration. This prohibition then in referring to the history of our state, originated in what may properly be called the slave period. It belongs to that period when piratical craft floated upon our waters, and our city of Newport was the great slave mart of New England. It belonged to the period when slaves found abroad after nine o'clock in the evening were confined in a cage until morning and then publicly whipped. It belonged to the period when the duties on imported slaves furnished means to pave the street leading to our State House, and when a bounty was offered for crows, black-birds, gray-squirrels, rats, old wolves and wild cats. The abolition of slavery is now complete, not only in Rhode Island but throughout the length and breadth of our country. The whipping-post has given way to less barbarous modes of punishment. The old wolves and the wild cats have been swept away by the tide of civilization or forced to seek some more sequestered spot, but this section still remains upon our statute book, a monument to prejudice and a relic of a less enlightened age. And until the colored people shall make for themselves a name and a place in the communities in which they dwell, that they may be allowed to stand with the white people, equal before the law, and to have the same opportunity. They are loyal to this country and this union. They have no mother country with which to divide their affections, but they are Americans in the strictest sense of that word, and have established their right to equality upon many a bloody field, fighting with us for the preservation of our common country. Who ever heard, during the war of the rebellion, or since, of a disloyal colored man, or of one who from fear or hope of reward ever betrayed a fleeing prisoner, or neglected to aid and assist him to the best of his ability in making good his escape. Sufficient evidence of the falsity of such a theory may be found in the fact that during the palmy days of slavery at the South, intercourse between blacks and whites upon the plantations was encouraged, in order that the property of the masters might be increased.

We have in our state a considerable number of respectable colored people, to whom this law is offensive, and who justly regard it as a discrimination against them. They do not desire to intermarry with the white people, but they feel that all legal restrictions should be removed and that they should be allowed to stand upon the same footing as other citizens. 1 appeal to the members of this house to throw aside their prejudices, to brave the sneers and taunts of the narrow minded, to strike from our statutes this relic of oppression, and to seek to assist and encourage the colored citizens of this state rather than deprive or offend them. Ever remembering that, and also the strong appeal from the strong argument of the closing debate, the General

Assembly had to yeald to law and justice for our dignity, that such a disgraceful law should be wiped from the statute book.

APPEAL.

In the year 1747 slaves on board a Rhode Island ship, Capt. Beers, rose and murdered the captain and crew, except two mates, who swam ashore. In 1731, Capt. George Scott, of Rhode Island, returning from Guinea with a cargo of slaves, they rose up and murdered the crew. Capt. Gibbs of Newport was one of the biggest slavers ever known. Capt. Townsend who lived on Brown street, Providence, was caught with a load of slaves. Readers, I give you some reasons why this law should be repealed. Because it was placed on the Statute book by such men for no other purpose than to reap corruption on innocent women. And when this thing was thoroughly discussed in the House of Representatives, in 1880, the christian community just got their eyes opened to the degraded purpose for which it was placed there. Lawyer Tillinghast, of Pawtucket, acknowledged in the Senate that he did not know Rhode Island was so base as to be the first to put such a law upon the Statute book, and all the other states, especially virginia, copied it from Rhode Island, to carry on this outrage upon virtuous women. He raised up his voice like a trumpet and said : away with such a law. Let the names of these great heroes and patriots of civilization and christianity, in the House of Representatives, which I have given the reader on page seventy-five of this work, be handed down to all generations hereafter, to be immortalized in the name of this great republic.

THE GRIEVANCE OF THE COLORED PEOPLE.

To the Editor of the Journal :

I see you have opened your columns very freely during the winter to criticisms on the Marriage Bill. So I beg leave, if you please, to give me a few lines in your columns, as you and the public at large do not understand our grievances upon this point. We petitioned to the General Assembly, as citizens of the State, and in common with other men, to repeal Section 6, Chapter 149, of the Revised Statutes, because it was, we thought, the last remnant of slavery in Rhode Island, so that the next generation might not find such a disgraceful law upon her Statute book. We say now, and always shall say, that it is better to marry than to live in such a disgraceful state as many are now living in.

It is not the line of color we are now contending on, for that line and the marriage question sink into insignificance before the rebukes we have received from Mr. Tobey and Mr. Pierce and Mr. Clark and Mr. Cross. If those gentlemen had merely voted against the bill we would not have said a word, but when those gentlemen stepped down from their high position of duty and used such language as they did, saying that if that law was repealed the next thing you would see running about the streets would be apes and baboons, and using all other mean language that they could, it is adding insult to injury, and it is this, and this alone, which has roused the indignation of the colored people, and should rouse the indignation of every lady and gentleman throughout the length and breadth of this land.

Yours respectfully,

GEORGE HENRY.

This is my first card, which the Journal took advantage of, and heaped all kinds of misrepresentations upon me, and would not give me an opportunity to defend myself through their columns, which I and everybody else thought was very unjust. I was compelled to resort to other means, when the editor of the Evening Telegram was kind and gentlemanly enough to open his columns for a free fight, as the Journal was full every day of race and color. I attacked him on both lines as follows:

GEORGE VS GEORGE.

What was the color of the first man? Some conundrums for the Journal to answer. The reason Tobey is opposed by the colored people.

To the editor of the Journal.

I was very sorry when you would not publish my

card. Hundreds of people have told me that you would not publish anything only on one side of the question. I have defended you on this point until you would not publish my card. I think it was a providential thing that you forced me to go to an editor who opens his columns for every man to have fair play. I have not had any answer to the above questions. I am waiting patiently for one.

Suffer me to say one word in regard to public school matters. I should do injustice to myself and to the three heroic women, who when nearly all the men backed down, came to my rescue and gave me new vigor in fighting successfully the repeal of the the law prohibiting equal school rights, namely Mrs. Amer, wife of Hon. S. G. Ames, Mrs. John E. Church and Mrs. Waugh. These names I wish handed down as a memorial to the last of posterity.

Mr. Editor, I see that you are very much displeased with us for excluding your reporter from our meetings. We did it for peace. Now I will tell you and the world the reason, and the sole reason, why we did it. We petitioned to the General Assembly to repeal Section 6, Chapter 149, of the Revised Statutes, and the next morning the first thing we saw in the Journal was something about the marriage between the negroes and whites, and of all of our meetings and caucuses. That and the color line was always in your reports. Now I say, sir, that we never discussed the question in any of our meetings, with the exception of one, and that was discussed by Messrs. Jefferson and Ballou, in the Police Station, and never anywhere else to my knowledge. Upon that issue it was only through the efforts of Mr. Eldrich, of Mount Zion Church, and myself, that Jefferson and Ballou were prevented from passing their resolutions for drawing out from the republican party, and establishing an independent party, and when we found that we were so misrepresented, and that it created feelings in the community that ought not to have existed, we excluded the reporter upon this ground alone. I leave the public to decide whether I am right or wrong.

Mr. Editor, since you will have this vexed marriage question before the public, let us discuss it. From 1784 to 1830 Rhode Island owned slaves, but in those days people were not as much enlightened as they are now. We made one step further in civilization when we established mixed schools. The great howl then arose, that the children would be fighting along the streets, and there would be continual dissentions. The result has just been the other way. We want to make one more step in civilization and christianity. The great howl comes up now: Do you want your daughter to marry a negro? I answer for myself. I don't want your daughters, because I have as good a wife as I want. I am fighting for the great principle of virtue. That black, odious, outrageous law was put there by the slaveholders, to cover up their fornications. Ninety-nine per cent. of all the mixing that is done is done by white men. More especially by slaveholders. The slave states copied that black law from Rhode Island, more especially Virginia, for she went into raising the mixed breeds. Some as pretty and virtuous women as the sun ever shown upon would be set on the block, and sold for nothing else but to make prostitutes of them, to the highest bidder. This I have seen with my own eyes, and this is the law which the Journal has such a particular love for. If I was editor of a paper it never should be blackened by upholding a law to support such fornication. I know, and thousands know, the disgrace that it has brought upon us. Now let us all pray that the great wave of public opinion may sweep it from the Statute Book, not only in the State of Rhode Island, but through the length and breadth of the land, and let purity take its place. You have filled your columns with word races. I hold that there is but one race of men, and I take my start from Adam, and I build my foundation from part of the 26th and 27th verses of the first chapter of Genesis. "Let us make man in our own image, after our likeness. So God created man in his own image, in the image of God created he him, male and female created he them." Also in the 7th verse of the 2d chapter of Genesis, which reads as follows : "And the Lord God framed man of the dust of the ground, and breathed into his nostrils the breath of life, and man became a living soul." This is my foundation. Now I hold that from Adam to the flood there was but one people, and all of one language. At the flood God destroyed every man except Noah and his three sons and their wives. The ark that they were saved in landed on the top of Mount Ararat. After this they began to build a tower to reach to heaven, for which God confounded their language, so that they did not understand each other. They were scattered thus over all the face of the earth in families, which we call tribes, and from wild tribes, becoming civilized and united they have become as nations.

Mr. Editor, here we stand with the bible claiming that I sprang from the seed of Adam, and I feel proud that I did, for God said that everything he had made was very good. Now Mr. Editor, where did you get your race from? if it is a different race from mine. Please tell me and the world, and if you cannot answer this question, never let me hear any more howls from your paper about races. You have filled your columns with regard to color. Let us discuss that a little, as we have an opportunity now that we never had before. Mr. Editor, I will ask you one question, so that I may be satisfied and also the entire public. I know, sir, from your great and masterly power, that you are able to answer it. Now what was the color of Adam? Was he a red man, was he a brown man, or was he a light complexioned man, or was he a black man, or was he a yellow man? I demand an answer, because I have always thought that he was a brown skinned man, because he was taken from the earth, though I may be wrong in my ideas. Therefore I ask for light on that subject. I know he was not a white man, because he was taken from the ground, and as there is nothing white under the ground but the drifting snow. Any other white substance has a shade when compared with it. Did you ever see a man in your life that was not of some color. When you dress yourself neatly, turn and look in the glass and see if your face is not of some color. I ask you with all kindness, can you change these colors? I have as much right to find fault with your light complexion as you have with my dark complexion. I hold that it is God himself who makes these different colors. If you look over Webster's dictionary you will see that white is not a color, and that black is destitute of light. Therefore all colors must be between those two mediums. I want to ask you one more question. Will you please to travel the length and breadth of your city, and you will find horses of all shades and colors, and of different shape and style, presently you will throw your eyes on a black horse, and if you can prove to me and the world that he is not a horse, then sir, you can prove the black man is not a man, and the argument will be yours, and if not, sir, the argument is mine, and never let me hear any more arguments in your paper on the color line. Sir, you have forced me to discuss this question, and I expect to receive great light on all these questions I have asked you, from your masterly pen, for I believe that there is no man living who is a better editor.

I want to say a few words to the public at large. When I put my card in the Journal, on the 13th, I was so provoked, because we were so badly represented, I merely said Mr. Cross, and I see that the Journal has taken advantage of that and would not publish my card, so that I could rectify my mistake, and I realy did not know my mistake until the editor of the Telegram published my card. Then I was asked if I meant Mr. Cross of Westerly. I answered that I did not, for I knew him in the Senate for the last three or four years, and I never heard him make a speech in my life. If the Journal had published my card this mistake would have been rectified long ago. Now sir, I will give the full name of the man I mean, as it was handed to me. It was I. W. C. Cross. That was the man I heard say that he would defeat the Niggers if they ever come here. He is the man and the only man I have reference to, and if the name is not correct it is not my fault, and that ends that controversy.

I have nothing against any man, except those who have spoken so disparangly of the colored race, and no one else. I mean reform and nothing else. The

Journal is solely responsible for all this discussion, because it would not publish my card when I wished to correct my mistake in the name.

Yours respectfully,

GEORGE HENRY.

THE SUBJECT OF COLONIZING.

At a meeting which convened in the District of Columbia, for the express purpose of agitating the subject of colonizing us in some part of the world, Mr. Clay was called to the chair, and having been seated a little while, he rose and spoke in substance as follows : Says he, "that class of the mixed population of our country, colored people, were peculiarly situated, they neither enjoyed the immunities of free men nor were they subjected to the incapacities of slaves, but partook in some degree of the qualities of both, from their condition and the unconquerable prejudices resulting from their color." And this was christian America. Here was where the colonization society started from—from a poor orphan boy, who had not clothes to wear nor bread to eat. But when the slaveholder found a person in Henry Clay to do their dirty work, a society, some of all villinous, they made laws and drove out the freemen, and took their property and made themselves rich. That is the principle of the colonization society down to the present. At a public dinner given him at Fowler's Garden, Lexington, Kentucky, Henry Clay delivered a public speech, to a very large concourse of people, in the concluding clause of which he says: "And now my friends and fellow citizens, I cannot part from you on possibly the last occasion of my ever publicly addressing you without reiterating the expression of my thanks from a heart overflowing with gratitude. I came among you, now more than thirty years ago, an orphan boy, penny-less, a stranger to you all, without friends, without the favor of the great. You took me up, cherished me, protected me, honored me. You have constantly poured upon me a bold and unbated stream of innumerable favors." These are the favors the great christian American has upheld and supported such a man as Henry Clay, and ministers of the pulpit, one of them said in the Capitol of the United States, when they were organizing this colonizing society, which I consider the sum of villinous, because it was got up by the ministers, the lower we can keep them on the line of brutes the better we can manage them. This is the language of christian ministers, sitting in the Capitol of the United States of America. Let principle, truth and righteousness cover our land, taking the Bible in one hand, the stars and stripes, our flag, in the other, and taking God for our standard, she will stand amongst the proud nations of the earth.

Sketch of Enslavement of the Blacks in the New World.

It is well known to the christian world that Bartholomew Lascasas, that very, very notoriously avaricious catholic priest, or preacher and adventurer, with Columbus, in his second voyage, proposed to his countrymen, the Spaniards, in Hispaniola, to import the African from the Portuguese settlement in Africa, to dig up gold and silver, and work their plantations for them. To effect which he made a voyage thence to Spain, and opened the subject to his master, Ferdinand, then in declining health, who listened to the plan, but who died soon after and left it in the hands of his successor, Charles the V. This wretch Lascasas, the preacher, succeeded so well in his plans of oppression, that in 1503 the first blacks had been imported into the new world. Elated with this success, and stimulated by sordid avarice only, he importuned Charles V, in 1511, to grant permission to a Flemish merchant to import 4,000 blacks at one time. Thus we see through the instrumentality of a pretended preacher of the gospel of Jesus Christ, our common master, our wretchedness first commenced in America, where it has been continued from 1503 to this day, 1829.

Now let us give a little history. In September,
1620, the Dutch Gallery, which was a regular pirate,
commanded by a Spaniard. She was stranded on
one of the West India Islands, and while there she
made acquaintance with these free colored people.
She got forty-five of them on board and then ran
away with them, and made harbor at Jamestown,
Virginia, and there she sold them to Spaniards who
had been trying to establish colonies for sixteen
years, and was in the act of giving up. The Spaniard's found them just the kind of people they could
make slaves of, and they petitioned to England with,
the sanction of the Pilgrims, who landed on Pilgrim's
Rock, December 22d, 1620, in four months after
the blacks landed in Jamestown, Virginia. They
then petitioned to England to grant them a charter
to run slaves from Africa, and they bought up all
vessels, some that were not sea-worthy, and all the
nation of Europe emptied their prisons of all the
thieves and robbers that were in them, with the understanding that they should run those vessels and
form a regular army in Africa, to catch all the slaves
to run them to all parts of Europe, to enrich their
country, all parts except Russia, she is not guilty of
that horrible crime.

Now sir, the South was settled by the Spaniards.
The Bible and this free education was never allowed
there until 1860, when the Rebublicans came into
power, and opened all the prison doors, and free

education, free Bible and free press. Was it any wonder that the black man did not make any progress equal to the white man, when the North and South, with the army and navy, barred out every avenue and made it a penalty of death by law to even read or write, or learn a trade. Now I hold that since the republicans have given them a chance under some degree they have made the greatest advancement of any other people known in the world. I dare any man to contradict that. I hold that Fred Douglass was the greatest man on this continent, for the chances he has had. When he was born mob law ruled from this country to the other. He was twenty-five years old before he could say his alphabet, but he soon came to be editor of a paper called North Star, which gave terror to the South.

Jamaica, the chief of the British West India Islands, was discovered by Columbus, on his second voyage, in May, 1494, and was taken from Spain by the English in May, 1855, during the reign of Oliver Cromwell, it thus became an appendage to the British crown, after it had been in the possession of Spain for one hundred and forty-six years. The number of slaves on the island at this time was about fifteen hundred. Morgan, a notorious pirate and buccaneer, was knighted and made governor of the island in 1670. Lord Vaughan succeeded Morgan and under his administration the African company was formed and the slave trade legalized.

Africans were imported in large numbers, and the development of the natural resources of Jamaica greatly increased the wealth of the planters. The number of slaves annually imported into the island amounted to sixteen thousand. So within thirty years the slave population had increased from ninety-nine thousand to upwards of two hundred thousand, whilest the total numerical strength of the whites did not exceed sixteen thousand. Now colored men why was this so. It was prejudice that kept you in slavery not the whites. Prejudice was what destroyed the carthaginians.

THE BOSTON MASSACRE.

March 5th, 1770 may be regarded as the first act
in the great drama of the American Revolution.
The presence of the British soldiers in King street,
excited the patriotic indignation of the people, but
it was not for the wise and prudent to be first to act
against the encroachments of arbitrary power. They
rushed to King street and were fired upon by Captain Preston's company. Crispus Attuck was the
first to fall. Samuel Gray and Jonas Caldwell were
killed on the spot. The first American man to fall
in defence of liberty was a black man. Three days
after, on the 8th, a public funeral took place, and
marched in columns six deep to the middle burying
ground, where the four victims were deposited in
one grave, over which a stone was placed, with the
following inscription :

> Long as in freedom's cause the wise contend,
> Dear to your country shall your fame extend.
> While to the world the lettered stone shall tell,
> Where Caldwell, Attuck, Gray and Maverick fell.

The anniversary of this event was publicly commem-
orated, in Boston, by an oration and other exercises
every year until after our national independence was

achieved. The fourth of July was then substituted for the fifth of March, as the more proper day for general celebration.

In those days there was no prejudice among the whites. There were one hundred thousand blacks in the Revolutionary War under arms, side by side with his countryman—fought in every battle on sea or land. The watchword then was liberty. Nearly a million blacks were scattered all over the country clearing up land and raising food and clothes for the support of the army.

The battle of Red Bank and the battle of Rhode Island, on the 29th of August, 1778, entitle the blacks to perpetual honor, for these battles were fought by black men—regiment of Negro slaves ordered to be raised by the General Assembly, February 9th, 1878.

The capture of Major General Prescott, of the British army, on the 9th of July, 1777, was an occasion of rejoicing throughout the country. Prince, the valliant Negro, who seized that officer, ought always to be remembered, with honor for this important service. They landed about five miles from Newport and three-quarters of a mile from the house. They approached cautiously, avoiding the main guard, which was at some distance. The Colonel went foremost, with a stout, active Negro close behind him, and another at a short distance. The rest followed, so as to be near, but not seen. A single sentinel at the door saw and hailed the Colonel. He answered by exclaiming against and inquiring for rebel prisoners, but kept slowly advancing. The sentinel again challenged him and required the counter-sign. He said he had not the counter-sign, but amused the sentry by talking about rebel prisoners, and still advancing till he came within reach of the bayonet which he presented. The Colonel suddenly struck aside and seized him. He was immediately secured and ordered to be silent on pain of instant death. Meanwhile the rest of the men surrounding the house, the Negro with his head at the second stroke, forced a passage into it and then into the landlord's apartment. The landlord at first refused to give the necessary intelligence ; but at the prospect of instant death, he pointed to the General's chamber, which was instantly opened by the Negro's head, the Colonel, calling the General by name, told him he was a prisoner.

Another heroic deed of the Negro soldiers was when Col. Green was surprised and murdered near Points Bridge, New York, on the 14th of May, 1781. His colored soldiers heroicly defended him till they were cut to pieces, and the enemy reached him over the dead bodies of his faithful Negro's.

In the Southern Rights Convention, which assembled at Baltimore, June 8th, 1860, a resolution was adopted, calling on the Legislature to pass a law driving the colored people out of the state. Nearly every speaker took the ground that the free colored people must be driven out to make the slaves obedience more secure. Judge Mason, in his speech said, it is the thrifty and well to do negros that are seen by our slaves that make them dissatisfied.

This is another heroic deed of the negro, William Tillman, captures the S. G. Waring, in the month of June, 1861. The Waring's head is turned towards New York with the stars and stripes flying. The S. G. Waring arrives in the port of New York, under the command of William Tillman, the negro patriot. The Federal Government awarded to Tillman the sum of six thousand dollars as prize money for the capture of the schooner.

General Jackson's Proclamation to the Negros.

Through a mistaken policy you have heretofore been deprived of a participation in the glorious struggle for national rights, in which our country is engaged. This no longer shall exist.

As sons of freedom, you are now called upon to defend our most inestimable blessing. As Americans, your country looks with confidence to her adopted children for a valorous support as a faithful return for the advantages enjoyed under her mild and equitable government. As fathers, husbands and brothers, you are summoned to rally round the standard of the Eagle to defend all which is dear in existence.

Your country, although calling for your exertions, does not wish you to engage in her cause without amply remunerating you for the services rendered. Your intelligent minds are not to be led away by false representations. Your love of honor would cause you to dispise the man who should attempt to deceive you. In the sincerity of a soldier, and the language of truth I address you.

To every noble hearted, generous freeman of color, volunteering to serve during the present contest with Great Britain, and no longer, there will be paid the same bounty in money and lands, now received by the white soldiers of the United States, viz: one hundred and twenty dollars in money, and one hundred and sixty acres of land.

The non-commissioned officers and privates will also be entitled to the same monthly pay and daily rations, and clothes, furnished to any American soldier.

On enrolling yourselves in companies, the Major General Commanding will select officers for your government from your white fellow-citizens. Your non-commissioned officers will be appointed from among yourselves.

Due regard will be paid to the feelings of freemen and soldiers. You will not by being associated with white men in the same corps be exposed to improper comparisons or unjust sarcasm. As a distinct, independent battalion, or regiment, pursuing the path of glory, you will undivided receive the applause and gratitude of your countrymen.

To assure you of the sincerety of my intention and my anxiety to engage your invaluable services to our country, I have communicated my wishes to the Governor of Louisiana, who is fully informed as to the manner of enrollment, and will give you every necessary information on the subject of this address.

ANDREW JACKSON,
Major General Commanding.

Three months later Gen. Jackson addressed the same troops as follows:

To the men of color, soldiers from the shores of Mobile. I collected you to arms, I invited you to share in the perils and to divide the glory of your white countrymen. I expected much from you, for I was not uninformed of those qualities which must render you so forminable to an invading foe. I knew that you could endure hunger and thirst, and all the hardships of war. I knew that you loved the land of your nativity, and like ourselves you had to defend all that is most dear to man, but you surpass my hopes. . I have found in you, united to these qualities, that noble enthusiasm which impels to great deeds.

Soldiers, the President of the United States shall be informed of your conduct on the present occasion, and the voice of the Representatives of the American nation shall applaud your valor, as your general now praises your ardor. But the brave are united, and if he finds us contending with ourselves it will be for the prize of valor and fame, its noblest reward.—[Niles' Register, vol. vii, pp. 345-346.]

Extract from a Letter, Etc.

Black men served in the navy with great credit to themselves, receiving the commendation of Com. Perry and other brave officers.

The following is an extract of a letter from Nathaniel Shaler, commander of the private armed schooner "Gen. Tompkins," to his agent in New York, dated at sea, Jan. 1, 1813:

"Before I could get our light sails in, almost before I could turn round, I was under the guns, not of a transport, but of a large frigate, and not more than a quarter of a mile from her. Her first broadside killed two men and wounded six others. My officers conducted themselves in a way that would have done honor to a more permanent service. The name of one of my poor fellows who was killed ought to be registered in the book of fame, and remembered with reverence as long as bravery is considered a virtue. He was a black man by the name of John Johnson. A twenty-four pound shot struck him in the hip and took away all the lower part of his body. In this state the poor brave fellow lay on the deck, and several times exclaimed to his shipmates: "Fire away my boys, no haul a color down.""

The other was also a black man, by the name of John Davis, and was struck in much the same way. He fell near me, and several times requested to be thrown overboard, saying he was only in the way of others."

When America has such tars she has little to fear from the tyrants of the ocean.

In 1620 a fleet of eighteen ships, under the command of Sir Robert Mansel, Vice-Admiral, was despatched to punish Algiers. It returned without being able, in the language of the times, to destroy those hellish pirates. It was in the year 1620, dear to all the descendants of the Pilgrims of Plymouth Rock, as an epoch of freedom, while an English fleet was seeking the emancipation of Englishmen, held in bondage by Algiers. The first liberation of the white American slavery was September 5, 1795. Their emancipation was purchased at the cost of more than seven hundred thousand dollars. A thrill of joy went through the land when it was announced that a vessel had left Algiers, having on board all the American captives, now happily at liberty. Three separate times Tripoli was attacked, and at last, on the 4th of June, 1805, entered into a treaty by which the freedom of three hundred American slaves was secured, on the payment of sixty thousand dollars, and it was provided that in the event of future war between the two countries, prisoners should not be reduced to slavery but should be ex-

changed rank for rank, and if there were any defic-
iency on either side it should be made up at the
rate of five hundred Spanish dollars for each captain,
three hundred dollars for each mate and supercargo,
and one hundred dollars for each seaman. Thus
did our country after successes, not without what is
called the glory of arms, again purchase with money
the emancipation of white citizens.

SLAVERY IN MODERN TIMES.

In the early periods of modern Europe, slavery
was a general custom, which yielded only gradually
to the humane influences of christianity. Fair haired
Saxon slaves, from distant England, arrested the
attention of Pope Gregory, in the markets of Rome,
and were by him hailed as angels. A law of so virtuous a king as Alfred, ranks slaves with horses and
oxen. Directly opposite to the Irish coast he says
there is a seaport called Bristol, the inhabitants of
which frequently sent into Ireland to sell those
people whom they had bought up throughout England. A boy was stolen from Scotland, who after
six years of bondage succeeded in reaching his
home, entering the church he returned to Ireland,
preached Christianity, and as St. Patrick became the
patron saint. Philip le Bel of France, grandson of
St. Louis, in 1296, presented his brother Charles,
Count of Valois, with a Jew, and paid three hundred
livres for another Jew, as if Jews were at the time

chattels to be given away or bought. Admiral de Kuyter, in 1661, enforced at Algiers the emancipation of several hundred Christian slaves. The inconsistency which we have before remarked appears also in these two powers, both while using their best endeavors for the freedom of their white people were cruelly engaged selling blacks into distant American slavery, as if every word of reprobation fastened upon the piratical slave driving Algiers, did not return in eternal judgment against themselves.

American White Slaves.

Masters of vessels were lodged together and indulged with a table by themselves, though a small iron ring was attached to one of their legs, to denote that they were slaves. Seamen were taught, and obliged to work at the trade of carpenter, blacksmith or stone-mason, from six in the morning till four in the afternoon, without intermission, except for half an hour at dinner. Here one of the American vessels was captured that was on her way to Africa, to buy slaves, they were captured themselves and made slaves. Here is the price they brought.

Crew of the ship Dolphin, of Philadelphia, captured July 30, 1785. Here is the price of American slavery:

Richard O'Brien, master,-	-	$2,000
Andrew Montgomery, mate,	-	1,500
Jacob Tessanier, French,	-	2,000

William Patterson, seaman,   - $1,500
Philip Solan,   "   -   725
Peleg Loring,   "   -   725
John Robertson,   "   -   725
James Hull,   "   -   725

Crew of the schooner Maria, of Boston, captured July 25, 1785 :

Isaac Stevens, master,   -   - $2,000
Alexander Forsythe, mate,   -   1,500
James Catheart, seaman,   -   900
George Smith,   "   -   725
John Gregory,   "   -   725
James Hermit,   "   -   725

EX-REBEL GENERAL ROGER A. PRYOR,

ON THE

PAST, PRESENT AND FUTURE OF THE NEGRO.

(FROM THE NEW YORK SUN.)

Gen. Roger A. Pryor delivered an eloquent address on Tuesday night, Dec. 9, before the Long Island Historical Society, in the chapel of the Packer Institute New York. His theme was "The Negro, his Past, Present and Future," and for more than an hour his earnest words kept a large and captivated audience intensely interested. General Pryor said:

In proportion as the negro shall be careful, prudent and industrious, he shall add to the material wealth of the country, and in just such proportion as he advances in mental culture, and in the building up of his moral nature he shall contribute to the elevation of society at large. But if he shall prove to be idle, improvident, immoral and vicious, he shall be a pest to society and a curse to himself and his kind.

The destiny of the individual depends largely, if not chiefly, on his inherited characteristics; and of all men none is so little beholden to past history as the black man. The history of his race is one long, sad story of lamentation and woe, of misery and oppression. No noble deeds of a noble ancestry illumine the page. It is all gloom and darkness and degradation. At the birth of his race everything was against him. The climate of his native land was enervating, and the soil such as demanded no manly toil to make it yield him food. For countless ages he groped in ignorance, until at last the Egyptians came and enslaved him. Thenceforth he was the thrall of earth. He became identified with us as the victim of a system of slavery for which the merchant of the North was as fully responsible as the planter of the South.

When emancipation came it found him ignorant, idle and improvident, and totally unfit for the change in his condition. Suddenly ushered upon the arena of life to struggle for existence, with the strongest nation in the world, he was looked upon with little favor by the one-half who had come to grief in the contest, and with but little more by the other, to whom he owed his freedom. It was confidently predicted that under the new order of things he would go from bad to worse, and at last become extinct, but he has shown an inherent strength of character not to be despised; and as a Southerner I say it, he is gradually making himself competent to the highest achievment of civilization. [Applause.] In the war he was not surpassed in courage by his fairer comrade; in devotion to the cause for which he fought he was not excelled; and what can equal the heroic fidelity with which he cared for and protected the defenceless wives and children of the Confederate soldiers who were struggling in the field to keep him in bondage? His virtues are his own; his vices are the result of the untoward circumstances that have always surrounded him.

The speaker then cited authorities to show that instead of dying out, as has been predicted, the negro race in the South was rapidly increasing in numbers.

In 1860 there were 3,953,700 slaves in the Southern States. In 1870 the census returns showed a population of 4,880,070 colored citizens. This increase of twenty per cent. is a sufficient rebuke of the contemptuous prediction of the black man's decay. The negro is also developing the resources of the country. In 1860 the cotton crop reached 3,550,000 bales; in 1866, the war having just closed, the yield was only 1,000,900 bales, but in 1872, the voluntary laborers, once slaves, but now freedmen, send to market 3,900,000 bales. As an evidence that the negroes of the South are improving morally, let me quote from reports touching the condition of thirty-one counties of Mississippi, which in 1865 had but nineteen colored schools, and in 1872 no fewer than 148. In 1865 only 564 marriage licenses had been issued to the blacks. In 1872 the number had increased to 3,950. I have great hopes for the negro. To be sure, the system of slavery was not the best school in which to learn the science of government, but we have not yet heard that negro congressmen were in any way implicated in the Credit Mobilier scandal, and I do not believe that the negro legislature of South Carolina was any more purchasable than the New York assembly during the days of the ring. [Applause.] What the negro wants is a chance to advance with the rest of mankind. In the North the theatres, the hotels, even the churches, are closed to him, and when he dies prejudice actually defies the equality of the grave, and forbids that his bones shall desecrate the sanctity of Greenwood, and Woodlawn, and Laurel Hill.

In conclusion, General Pryor predicted, that the extreme Southern States would become the home of the blacks,—that in fifty years they will be 10,000,000 strong, and that they will bring to our councils that patriotism which the memory of their later past must inspire.

Bequests to Educate Freedmen in the South.

The contest of the will of Daniel Hand, of Guilford, Conn., has been ended, and the estate, amounting to about $400,000, will soon be settled. The income of which is to be used for the education of the freedmen in the South. At the outbreak of the civil war, Mr. Hand left $130,000 with his old business partner, G. W. Williams, of Charleston, S. C. It was the honesty of Mr. Williams in the transaction which suggested to Mr. Hand the return of the sum to the South, as a gift to the freedmen, and to that great gift $400,000 will soon be added by his will, making $1,400,000 altogether.

There was another large sum given by a gentleman from Maryland, I cannot think of his name. May God bless the hand of all such givers of humanity.

Mr. Slattery, of Rhode Island, left a large sum for the education of the freedmen in the South. All honor to one of Rhode Island's sons. One million dollars, income only to be used, ($1,000,000.)

George Peabody also left a large sum to educate the freedmen in the South, two million dollars, ($2,000,000), one-third of which was to be used for the education of the freedmen.

THE COLORED SOLDIER.

Ives Post, No. 13, G. A. R., Crowded Steinway
Hall Last Night.

A Memorial Volume, the Gift of George Henry,
Presented to the Post.

It was an enthusiastic company which packed
Steinway hall last evening, at the twenty-sixth anniversary of Ives Post, No. 13, G. A. R. The event
of the evening was the presentation of a memorial
volume in which to keep the war records of the
members of the post. It was the gift of Mr. George
Henry, a venerable colored freedman. Among the
guests of the evening were Col. Daniel R. Ballou,
Junior Vice Department Commander of the State;
Department Chaplain Rev. Hopkins B. Cady, of
Newport; Past Department Commander John H. F.
Francis, Rev. J. B. Colbert, Rev. Joseph O. Johnson,
members of Department Commander Baker's staff,
and many other well-known G. A. R. men. De-
tachments were present from Ives corps, No. 11, and
Bucklin, Tower and Slocum posts, besides many
members of other posts and Sons of Veterans'

camps. Grand circle, No. 3, of the ladies of the G. A. R., also attended.

After a piano solo by Miss Wilson and prayer by Rev. J. B. Colbert, Commander James C. Lecompt delivered a brief address of welcome. Miss Wilson gave another solo and there was a recitation, "Union and Liberty," by Master R. E. Johnson.

In presenting the memorial volume, Col. Ballou, who spoke in behalf of the donor, assured the audience of the pleasure he had in performing that duty, and spoke in glowing terms of the bravery of the colored soldier in the great rebellion. In referring to the future of the colored race, he said that he believed they would not be wanting in devotion to their government. He then spoke of Coxey's army.

After a song by Prof. R. W. Marks, accompanied by Mr. Jefferson, the acceptance of the memorial by Col. John H. Monroe, in behalf of the post, was given in a few appropriate and feeling words.

Mr. Henry, who sat on the platform, was enthusiastically cheered, and made a speech in response. After more singing by Prof. Marks, and a recitation by Miss Nellie Dixon, Rev. Hopkins B. Cady spoke a few words for Department Commander Charles H. Baker, who was unavoidably absent.

Rev. J. B. Colbert made a spirited address on the patriotism of the colored citizen. Master Howard S. West recited the "Charge of the Light Brigade," and there were remarks by Past Commander Francis.

The exercises were concluded by the singing of "America" by the audience, and the benediction was pronounced by Rev. Joseph I. Johnson. James E. Johnson acted as master of the ceremonies. Light refreshments were served.—[Report from Providence daily paper.]

TO MY EXECUTORS.

This history of my life, which I have had published, I want my executors to distribute as follows. One copy to be given to every one to whom I have left a donation, leave half a dozen in my library, and the balance may be distributed as they think best.

GEORGE HENRY.